D0040758

VOGUE KNITTING

SOCKSTWO

on the go! ™

VOGUE KNITTING

SOCKSTWO

SIXTH&SPRING BOOKS
NEW YORK

SIXTH&SPRING BOOKS
233 Spring Street
New York, New York 10013

Library of Congress Cataloging-in-Publication Data

Vogue knitting socks two / [editor, Trisha Malcolm].
p. cm. -- (Vogue knitting on the go!)
ISBN 1-931543-14-3
1. Knitting--Patterns. 2. Socks. I. Title: Socks two. II. Malcolm, Trisha, 1960- III.
Series.

TT825 .V6472 2002
746.43'20432--dc21   2002021049

Manufactured in China

1 3 5 7 9 10 8 6 4 2

First Edition

TABLE OF CONTENTS

INTRODUCTION

In a world spent rushing from one place to the next, bustling from one project to another, we all need a way to unwind. Think about the little windows of opportunity that occur throughout your day: an endless wait in the doctor's office, the morning commute; even coming attractions at the movie theater. You'll see this "lost" time in a whole new light when your yarn and needles let you make it productive.

Socks Two is perfect for stolen moments on-the-go. Socks, afterall, are made to move. Small and portable, the projects featured on these pages slip into your bag without a second thought. They're the perfect way to experiment with new stitch patterns and color combinations, and to indulge in the wonder of luxury yarn without breaking the bank. From basic "Kid's Striped Socks" to fanciful Fair Isle designs and whimsical "Penguin Slipper Socks," the collection has something for everyone.

So treat your feet (and those of family members and friends) to one or more of these fabulous designs. The simple satisfaction of creating something of style and substance with your own two hands is sure to inspire.

So jump in feet first, grab your needles and get ready to **KNIT ON THE GO!**

THE BASICS

Socks, or "stockings" as some still call them, have been knit for hundreds of years all around the world. In many countries children are taught to knit socks at a young age. To those without the benefit of this experience, sock-knitting may appear sophisticated. Actually, "turning" a heel is an easy skill to master and the excitement of seeing the heel develop adds a certain momentum to sock-knitting. Socks can be constructed in all manners—knit in-the-round on double pointed needles or knit flat and then seamed—and just about any type of patterning can be incorporated into a sock's design. This book explores many variations and sets out the basics, so you can please your feet and the feet of those you love with beautiful socks.

SOCK CONSTRUCTION

Most of the socks in this book have been knit in rounds on a set of 4 or 5 double pointed needles (dpn). This eliminates seams at heels and toes, making them more comfortable for the wearer.

The toes are often woven together using the Kitchener stitch. The Kitchener stitch mimics a knit stitch, is neat, and provides an invisible seam (see page 15).

The few exceptions to circular sock knitting are the Slipper Socks, Domino Square Socks and Two-Needle Socks. The Slipper Socks begin with a flat knit sole and then are worked in rounds; the Domino Square Socks have separately knit squares that are joined in rounds. The Two-Needle Socks are knit as one entire flat piece.

Cuff

Most of the socks in this book begin with the cuff. Stitches are cast on to one needle, then divided onto three or four needles to work in rounds. This helps keep the stitches from twisting on the first round. For most socks, the number of stitches on the cuff will equal the number of stitches on the foot after the heel and instep shaping are completed.

Heel

After the cuff is the desired length, stitches are generally divided in half and shifted around the needles so that the center of the heel is the beginning of the cuff rounds. The remaining instep (front of foot) stitches are divided onto two needles to be worked later.

The heel is then worked straight (that is back and forth in rows), until it is the desired depth. The heel is then shaped with short rows into a V-shape or a curved U-shape.

Instep

To begin working in rounds again, as well as to join instep to heel, stitches are knit and repositioned again so that the round begins at the center of the heel (or sole). Stitches are picked up and knit along each side of the heel piece, joining heel and instep. Then the instep is shaped in a wedge shape, sometimes called a gusset, with decreases usually spelled out on the first and last needles only.

Foot

When the heel shaping is complete, the foot is worked straight, resuming original patterns, until the sock foot measures 1½ to 2"/4 to 5cm less than the desired length from the end of the heel to the tip of the toe.

Toe

Once again, if the stitches are not already in the correct alignment, they are shifted so that half the stitches are on Needle 2 and the other half of the stitches are divided onto Needles 1 and 3. Then double decreases are worked at each side edge of the toe to the required length.

SIZING

Sock sizing is as individual as shoe sizing. General sizing information is given with each set of instructions. Styles are categorized as woman's, man's, child's, infant's or adults, with a general length given.

The best approach to fit is to measure the foot of the wearer (from end of heel to end of toe) and knit the foot length accordingly. Individual taste and wearing style also help determine fit, whether it be a house sock, boot sock or dress sock.

YARN SELECTION

For an exact reproduction of the socks photographed, use the yarn listed in the materials section of the pattern. We've chosen yarns that are readily available in the U.S. and Canada at the time of printing. The Resources list on pages 86 and 87 provides addresses of yarn distributors. Contact them for the name of a retailer in your area.

YARN SUBSTITUTION

You may wish to substitute yarns. Perhaps you view small-scale projects as a chance to incorporate leftovers from your yarn stash, or the yarn specified may not be available in your area. You'll need to knit to the given gauge to obtain the knitted measurements with a substitute yarn (see "Gauge" on page 12). Be sure to consider how the fiber content of the substitute yarn will affect the comfort and the ease of care of your socks.

To facilitate yarn substitution, *Vogue Knitting* grades yarn by the standard stitch gauge obtained in Stockinette stitch. You'll find a grading number in the "Materials" section of the pattern, immediately following the fiber type of the yarn. Look for a substitute yarn that falls into the same category. The suggested gauge on the ball band should be comparable to that on the Yarn Symbols chart (below).

After you've successfully gauge-swatched a substitute yarn, you'll need to figure out how much of the substitute yarn the project requires. First, find the total length of the original yarn in the pattern (multiply number of balls by yards/meters per ball). Divide this figure by the new yards/meters per ball (listed on the ball band). Round up to the next whole number. The answer is the number of balls required.

FOLLOWING CHARTS

Charts are a convenient way to follow colorwork, lace, cable and other stitch patterns at a glance. *Vogue Knitting* stitch charts utilize the universal knitting language of "symbol-

YARN SYMBOLS

① **Fine Weight**
(29-32 stitches per 4"/10cm)
Includes baby and fingering yarns, and some of the heavier crochet cottons.

② **Lightweight**
(25-28 stitches per 4"/10cm)
Includes sport yarn, sock yarn, UK 4-ply and lightweight DK yarns.

③ **Medium Weight**
(21-24 stitches per 4"/10cm)
Includes DK and worsted, the most commonly used knitting yarns.

④ **Medium-heavy Weight**
(17-20 stitches per 4"/10cm)
Also called heavy worsted or Aran.

⑤ **Bulky Weight**
(13-16 stitches per 4"/10cm)
Also called chunky. Includes heavier Icelandic yarns.

⑥ **Extra-bulky Weight**
(9-12 stitches per 4"/10cm)
The heaviest yarns available.

GAUGE

It is always important to knit a gauge swatch, and it is even more so with socks as they are designed to fit the foot. If your gauge is too loose, you could end up with sloppy slipper-socks instead of anklets; if it's too tight, you could end up with a sock that has to be pulled over the heel using a shoehorn.

Making a flat gauge swatch for socks *knit* in the round will allow you to measure *gauge over* a 4"/10cm span that will lay flat for better *reading*. However, when a sock includes a complex *stitch* pattern knit in rounds, a circularly-knit *swatch* will test the gauge best and the practice will familiarize you with the pattern—cast on at least as many stitches required for the sock. The type of needles used—straight or double pointed, wood or metal—will influence gauge, so knit your swatch with the needles you plan to use for the project. Measure gauge as illustrated. Try different needle sizes until your sample measures the required number of stitches and rows. To get fewer stitches to the inch/cm, use larger needles; to get

more stitches to the inch/cm, use smaller needles.

Knitting in the round may tighten the gauge, so if you measured the gauge on a flat swatch, take another gauge reading after you begin your sock. When the sock measures at least 2"/5cm after the cuff, lay it flat and measure over the stitches in the center of the piece, as the side stitches may be distorted. Keep in mind that if you consciously try to loosen your tension to match the flat knit swatch you can prevent having to go up a needle size.

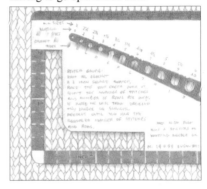

craft." When knitting in the round, read charts from right to left on every round, repeating any stitch and row repeats as directed in the pattern. When knitting back and forth in rows, read charts from right to left on right side (RS) rows and from left to right on wrong side (WS) rows. Posting a self-adhesive note under your working row is an easy way to keep track of your place on a chart.

COLORWORK KNITTING

Two main types of colorwork are explored in this book.

Intarsia

Intarsia is accomplished with separate bobbins of individual colors. This method is ideal for large blocks of color or for motifs that aren't repeated close together, such as the Striped Patchwork Socks. When changing colors, always pick up the new color and wrap it around the old color to prevent holes.

For smaller areas of color, such as the Striped Sheep Socks, duplicate stitch embroidery works best after the pieces are knit (see page 15).

Stranding

When motifs are closely placed, colorwork

is accomplished by stranding along two or more colors per row, creating "floats" on the wrong side of the fabric. This technique is sometimes called Fair Isle knitting after the traditional Fair Isle patterns composed of small motifs with frequent color changes.

To keep an even tension and prevent holes while knitting, pick up yarns alternately over and under one another across or around. While knitting, stretch the stitches on the needle slightly wider than the length of the float at the back to keep work from puckering.

When changing colors at the beginning of rows or rounds, carry yarn along for a few rows only, or cut yarn and rejoin when needed. It is important to keep the "floats" small and neat so that toes don't catch on them when pulling on socks.

LACE

Lace knitting provides a feminine touch to some of the socks featured in this book. Knitted lace is formed with "yarn overs," which create an eyelet hole, in combination with decreases that create directional effects. To make a yarn over (yo), merely pass the yarn over the right-hand needle to form a new loop (see page 16). Decreases are worked as k2tog, ssk or SKP depending on the desired slant and are spelled out specifically with each instruction. On the row or round that follows the lace or eyelet detail, each yarn over is treated as one stitch. If you're new to lace knitting, it's a good idea to count the stitches at the end of each row or round. Making a gauge swatch in the stitch pattern enables you to practice a new lace pattern. Instead of binding off the swatch, place the final row on a holder, as the bind off tends to pull in the stitches and distort the gauge.

BLOCKING

Blocking is an all-important finishing step in the knitting process. Most sock styles will retain their best shape by pressing flat with a slight fold line down the center of the instep and heel. When working flat insteps or cuffs in rows instead of rounds (such as the Striped Patchwork Socks), pin and block flat areas first before joining.

Wet Block Method

Pin pieces to measurements on a flat surface and lightly dampen using a spray bottle. Allow to dry before removing pins.

Steam Block Method

Pin pieces to measurements or smooth into place with hands. Steam lightly, holding the iron approximately 2"/5cm above the knitting. Do not press an iron onto any knitting, as it will flatten the stitches.

CARE

Hand-knit socks require the same care as hand-knit sweaters. Hand wash one pair of socks at a time for best results. Use cold water and dissolve soap flakes or a mild detergent before immersing the socks. Let socks soak for 5-10 minutes, then gently squeeze suds through, never pulling or rubbing. Rinse with plenty of water until all soap is washed away. Gently squeeze out water then blot between layers of towels to absorb any excess. Lay flat to dry, pressing to original measurements with hands.

FINISHING TECHNIQUES

The socks in this book make use of embroidered, knitted and crocheted embellishments as well as trims made with yarn. Wrap & Turn (w&t) shapes the heel of the Penguin Slipper Socks; the twisted cord is pulled through eyelet rows on the Medieval Knee Socks; and Kitchener Stitch makes a seamless toe for almost every sock. You'll also want to refer to illustrations at the end of this section for other useful techniques.

SHORT ROW SHAPING	JOINING ROUNDS
"WRAP AND TURN"	DOUBLE-POINTED NEEDLES

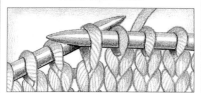

1 To prevent holes in the piece and create a smooth transition, wrap a knit stitch as follows: With the yarn in back, slip the next stitch purlwise.

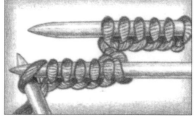

1 Cast on required number of stitches on the first needle, plus one extra. Slip extra stitch to next needle as shown. Continue in this way, casting on the required number of stitches on the needle (or, cast on all stitches onto one needle, then divide them evenly over the other needles).

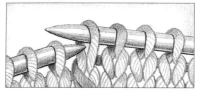

2 Move the yarn between the needle to the front of the work.

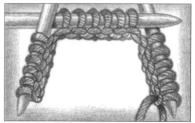

2 Arrange needles as shown, with cast-on edge facing center of triangle (or square).

3 Slip the same stitch back to the left needle. Turn the work, bringing the yarn to the purl side between the needles. One stitch is wrapped.

3 Place a stitch marker after the last cast-on stitch. With the free needle, knit the first cast-on stitch, pulling the yarn tightly. Continue knitting in rounds, slipping the marker before beginning each round.

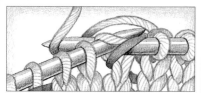

4 When you have completed all the short rows, you must hide the wraps. Work to just before the wrapped stitch. Insert the right needles under the wrap and knitwise into the wrapped stitch. Knit them together.

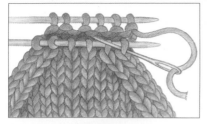

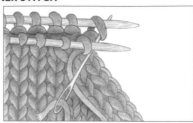

1 *Insert tapestry needle purlwise (as shown) through first stitch on front needle. Pull yarn through, leaving that stitch on knitting needle.*

2 *Insert tapestry needle knitwise (as shown) through first stitch on back needle. Pull yarn through, leaving stitch on knitting needle.*

3 *Insert tapestry needle knitwise through first stitch on front needle, slip stitch off needle and insert tapestry needle purlwise (as shown) through next stitch on front needle. Pull yarn through, leaving this stitch on needle.*

4 *Insert tapestry needle purlwise through first stitch on back needle. Slip stitch off needle and insert tapestry needle knitwise (as shown) through next stitch on back needle. Pull yarn through, leaving this stitch on needle.*
Repeat steps 3 and 4 until all stitches on both front and back needles have been grafted. Fasten off and weave in end.

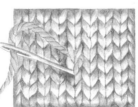

DUPLICATE STITCH

Duplicate stitch covers a knit stitch. Bring the needle up below the stitch to be worked. Insert the needle under both loops one row above and pull it through. Insert it back into the stitch below and through the center of the next stitch in one motion, as shown.

There are different ways to make a yarn over. Which method to use depends on where you are in the stitch pattern. If you do not make the yarn over in the right way, you may lose it on the following row, or make a yarn over that is too big. Here are the different variations:

Between two knit stitches: Bring the yarn from the back of the work to the front between the two needles. Knit the next stitch, bringing the yarn to the back over the right-hand needle, as shown.

Between a knit and a purl stitch: Bring the yarn from the back to the front between the two needles. Then bring it to the back over the right-hand needle and back to the front again, as shown. Purl the next stitch.

Between a purl and a knit stitch: Leave the yarn at the front of the work. Knit the next stitch, bringing the yarn to the back over the right-hand needle, as shown.

Between two purl stitches: Leave the yarn at the front of the work. Bring the yarn to the back over the right-hand needle and to the front again, as shown. Purl the next stitch.

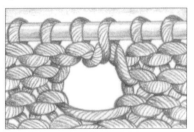

Multiple yarn overs (two or more): Wrap the yarn around the needle, as when working a single yarn over, then continue wrapping the yarn around the needle as many times as indicated. Work the next stitch of the left-hand needle. On the following row, work stitches into the extra yarn overs as described in the pattern. The illustration at right depicts a finished yarn over on the purl side.

KNITTING TERMS AND ABBREVIATIONS

approx approximately

beg begin(ning)

bind off Used to finish an edge and keep stitches from unraveling. Lift the first stitch over the second, the second over the third, etc. (UK: cast off)

cast on A foundation row of stitches placed on the needle in order to begin knitting.

CC contrast color

ch chain(s)

cm centimeter(s)

cont continu(e)(ing)

dc double crochet (UK: tr-treble)

dec decrease(ing)—Reduce the stitches in a row (knit 2 together).

dpn double pointed needle(s)

foll follow(s)(ing)

g gram(s)

garter stitch Knit every row. Circular knitting: knit one round, then purl one round.

hdc half-double crochet (UK: htr-half treble)

inc increase(ing)—Add stitches in a row (knit into the front and back of a stitch).

k knit

k2tog knit 2 stitches together

lp(s) loops(s)

LH left-hand

m meter(s)

M1 make one stitch—With the needle tip, lift the strand between last stitch worked and next stitch on the left-hand needle and knit into the back of it. One stitch has been added.

MC main color

mm millimeter(s)

no stitch On some charts, "no stitch" is indicated with shaded spaces where stitches have been decreased or not yet made. In such cases, work the stitches of the chart, skipping over the "no stitch" spaces.

oz ounce(s)

p purl

p2tog purl 2 stitches together

pat pattern

pick up and knit (purl) Knit (or purl) into the loops along an edge.

pm place marker—Place or attach a loop of contrast yarn or purchased stitch marker as indicated.

rem remain(s)(ing)

rep repeat

rev St st reverse Stockinette stitch—Purl right-side rows, knit wrong-side rows. Circular knitting: purl all rounds. (UK: reverse stocking stitch)

rnd(s) round(s)

RH right-hand

RS right side(s)

sc single crochet (UK: dc - double crochet)

sk skip

SKP Slip 1, knit 1, pass slip stitch over knit 1.

sl slip—An unworked stitch made by passing a stitch from the left-hand to the right-hand needle as if to purl.

sl st slip stitch (UK: single crochet)

ssk slip, slip, knit—Slip next 2 stitches knitwise, one at a time, to right-hand needle. Insert tip of left-hand needle into fronts of these stitches from left to right. Knit them together. One stitch has been decreased.

st(s) stitch(es)

St st Stockinette stitch—Knit right-side rows, purl wrong-side rows. Circular knitting: knit all rounds. (UK: stocking stitch)

tbl through back of loop

tog together

WS wrong side(s)

w&t wrap and turn

wyif with yarn in front

wyib with yarn in back

work even Continue in pattern without increasing or decreasing. (UK: work straight)

yd yard(s)

yo yarn over—Make a new stitch by wrapping the yarn over the right-hand needle. (UK: yfwd, yon, yrn)

* Repeat directions following * as many times as indicated.

[ ] Repeat directions inside brackets as many times as indicated.

Tuxedo toes

For Experienced Knitters

Kid's slipper socks have an easy-turn heel and a snug fit rib cuff combined with plenty of penguin-like details. Designed by Mary J. Saunders to delight your favorite child.

SIZES

Instructions are written for Child's size Small (5-6½). Changes for size Large (6½-8) are in parentheses.

KNITTED MEASUREMENTS

- Leg width 4½ (6)"/11.5 (15)cm
- Foot length 5½ (7½)"/14 (19)cm

MATERIALS

- 2 1¾oz/50g balls (each approx 131yd/120m) of K1C2, LLC *Crème Brûlée DK* (wool ③) in #908 grey (A)
- 1 ball in #909 black (B) and a small amount in #101 ecru (C)
- One set (4) size 5 (3.75mm) double pointed needles (dpn) or *size to obtain gauge*
- Stitch holders

GAUGE

20 sts and 28 rows/rnds to 4"/10cm over reverse St st using double strand of yarn and size 5 (3.75mm) dpn.
Take time to check gauge.

W & T

Wrap and turn (see page 14 for details).
Note Work with double strand of yarn except for wings, beak and duplicate st embroidery. Slipper is knit with A on wrong side (k side), then is turned to right side (p side) after sock is finished.

CUFF

With double strand of A using one needle, loosely cast on 28 (36) sts. Divide sts on 3 needles with 9 (12) sts on *Needle 1*, 9 (12) sts on *Needle 2* and 10 (12) sts on *Needle 3*. Join, taking care not to twist sts on needles. Mark end of rnd and sl marker every rnd. Work in k1, p1 rib for 2 (2½)"/5 (6.5)cm.

HEEL

Row 1 K 14 (18) sts and leave on needle for heel. Place rem 14 (18) sts on a st holder for instep.
Row 2 P13 (17), w&t.
Row 3 K12 (16), w&t
Row 4 P11 (15), w&t.
Row 5 K 10 (14), w&t.
Cont to work in this way having 1 less st each row until there are 4 (8) sts on last RS row.
Turn heel
Next row P5 (9), w&t.
Next row K6 (10), w&t. Then cont as foll:
Row 1 P6 (10), k1, w&t.
Row 2 P1, k6 (10), p1, w&t
Row 3 K1, p6 (10), k1, p1, w&t.
Row 4 K1, p1, k6 (10), p1, k1, w&t.
Row 5 P1, k1, p6 (10), k1, p2, w&t.
Row 6 K2, p1, k6 (10), p1, k2, w&t.

Row 7 P2, k1, p6 (10), k1, p3, turn.

Row 8 K3, p1, k6 (10), p1, k3.

FOOT

Rejoin to work in rnds, pm at beg of rnd as foll: **Next rnd** *Needle 1* K7 (9) sts from instep; *Needle 2* k7 (9) sts rem from instep; *Needle 3* work 14 (18) sts from heel, k the knit and p the purl sts. Cont working as established until foot measures 3 (4½)"/7.5 (11.5)cm from back of heel or 2½ (3)"/6.5 (7.5)cm less than total length of foot.

HEAD

Change to 2 strands B to complete foot.

Rnd 1 P18 (22), k6 (10), p4.

Rnd 2 K3 (5), p8, k6 (8), p1, k6 (10), p1, k3.

Rnd 3 K2 (4), p10, k5 (7), p1, k6 (10), p1, k3.

Rnd 4 K1 (3), p12, k4 (6), p1, k6 (10), p1, k3.

Rnd 5 K0 (2), p14, k3 (5), p1, k6 (10), p1, k3.

Rnd 6 K0 (1), p14 (16), k3 (4), p1, k6 (10), p1, k3.

Rep last rnd 6 (7) times more.

SHAPE TOE

Rnd 1 *Needle 1* K1, p2tog, p to end; *Needle 2* p to last 3 sts, p2tog tbl, k1; *Needle 3* k1, k2tog tbl, p1, k to last 4 sts, p1, k2tog, k1. **Rnd 2** *Needle 1* K1, p2tog, p to end; *Needle 2* p to last 3 sts, p2tog tbl, k1; *Needle 3* k1, k2tog tbl, k to last 3 sts, k2tog, k1.

Rep rnd 2 until there are 12 sts. **Next rnd** [K2tog] 6 times. Cut yarn and pull through rem 6 sts and draw up tightly and secure end. Turn sock to RS (purl side of fabric).

WINGS

(make 2 for each slipper)

With single strand A, cast on 14 (16) sts on one needle. Divide sts on 3 needles with 4 (6) sts on *Needle 1* and 5 sts on *Needle 2* and 3. Join, taking care not to twist sts on needle. Mark end of rnd and sl marker every rnd. K 3 (4) rnds. **Next (inc) rnd** K1, M1, k to last st, M1, k1. [Work 1 rnd even. Rep inc rnd] 1 (2) times—18 (22) sts. K 3 (4) rnds. **Rnd 1** K1, ssk, k to last 3 sts, k2tog, k1. **Rnd 2** Knit. Rep these 2 rnds 4 (6) times more— 8 sts rem. **Next rnd** [Ssk] twice, [k2tog] twice. Cut yarn and pull through rem 4 sts and draw up tightly and secure end.

FINISHING

Block socks being careful not to flatten rib. Block wings flat. Sew wings to head and tack tip of wings at rib foll photo.

FACE

With single strand of C, embroider face in duplicate st embroidery foll chart for chosen size. With double strand B, make 2 French knots for eyes and place as indicated by the black circles on chart.

BEAK

With double strand of B, pick up and k 6 sts at center of face as indicated by (/) on chart. Divide sts on 3 needles and join. K 2 rnds. **Next rnd** [K2tog] 3 times. Cut yarn and pull through rem 3 sts and draw up tightly and secure end.

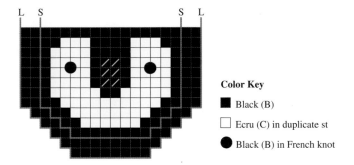

Color Key

■ Black (B)

☐ Ecru (C) in duplicate st

● Black (B) in French knot

DOMINO SQUARE SOCKS
Mitered mosaic

One large and eight small mitered squares form the basis of these unique colorful socks worked in alternating solid and rainbow-colored yarns. This winsome design is by Jaya Srikrishnan.

SIZES

Instructions are written for Woman's size Small. Changes for sizes Medium, Large and X-Large are in parentheses.

KNITTED MEASUREMENTS

- Leg width 7¼ (7½, 8, 8½)"/18.5 (19, 20.5, 21.5)cm
- Foot length 8½ (9, 9½, 10)"/21 (22.5, 24, 25.5)cm

MATERIALS

- 2 1¾oz/50g skeins (each approx 215yd/198m) of Stahl Wolle/Tahki•Stacy Charles, Inc. *Socka* (wool ①) in #50 navy (A)
- 1 1¾oz/50g skein (each approx 215yd/198m) of Lorna's Laces *Shepherd Sock* (wool ①) in #601 socknitters rainbow (B)
- 1 set (5) size 0 (2mm) double pointed needles (dpn) *or size to obtain gauge*
- 1 larger size needle, for binding off
- Stitch markers

GAUGE

36 sts and 48 rows/rnds to 4"/10cm over St st using size 0 (2mm) dpn.
Take time to check gauge.

W & T

Wrap and turn (see page 14 for details).

Note To work *RS join*, on a RS row, sl the last st knitwise wyif, with the LH needle, pick up the 2 lps of the edge st on the adjoining strip, sl the last st back to LH needle and p this st and the lps tog. Turn, sl the first st knitwise wyib and purl across row.

To work *WS join*, on a WS row, sl the last st knitwise wyib; with the LH needle, pick up the 2 lps of the edge st on the adjoining strip and k it; pass the sl st over. Turn, sl the first st purlwise and knit across row.

STITCH GLOSSARY

EYE OF PARTRIDGE ST

(even number of sts)
Row 1 *Sl 1, k1; rep from * to end.
Rows 2 and 4 Sl 1, purl to end.
Row 3 Sl 1, *sl 1, k1; rep from *, end k1.
Rep these 4 rows for eye of partridge st.

LARGE MITERED SQUARE—CHART 1

This square is placed on the top of the foot. Work back and forth in rows as foll:
With A, cast on 65 (69, 73, 77) sts, pm at center st (use removable marker).
Row 1 (RS) With A, knit.
Row 2 With A, k to center st, p1, k to end. Join B.
Row 3 With B, k to 1 st before center st, sl 2 sts as for k2tog without knitting them, k1, pass, the 2 sl sts over the k st (s2kp), k to end.

Row 4 With B, purl.

Rep these 4 rows foll chart until 1 st rem. Cut color B, leaving this st on needle, with color A and RS facing, pick up and k 31 (33, 35, 37) sts across the top of the mitered square for 32 (34, 36, 38) sts.

TOE

With A, work in St st on these sts for 7 (7, 7, 9) rows.

Toe shaping

Row 1 Knit. **Row 2** Sl 1, p to last st, w&t. **Row 3** Sl 1, k to last st, w&t. **Row 4** Sl 1, p to 1 st before wrapped st, w&t. **Row 5** Sl 1, k to 1 st before wrapped st, w&t. Rep rows 4 and 5 until there are 16 (16, 18, 18) sts at center with 8 (9, 9, 10) sts wrapped on each side of toe. Then, cont to work underside of toe as foll: **Next row** Sl 1, p to wrapped st, pick up with wrap and p2tog, turn. **Next row** Sl 1, k to wrapped st, pick up with wrap and k2tog tbl, turn. Rep these 2 rows until all wrapped sts are worked and there are 32 (34, 36, 38) sts on needle.

SOLE

Next row With A, p to last st, p last st tog with 1 st from side edge of mitered square. **Next row** With A, k to last st, k last st tog with 1 st from side of mitered square. Cont to work sole in this way until all sts are joined to mitered square.

Heel Flap

Cont on the 32 (34, 36, 38) heel sts with A only, work 31 (33, 35, 37) rows in eye of partridge st.

Turn heel

Cont in the eye of partridge pat while turning heel, work as foll:

Row 1 (RS) Sl 1, work 20 (21, 23, 24) sts in eye of partridge st, ssk, turn. **Row 2** Sl 1, work 10 (10, 12, 12), p2tog, turn. **Row 3** Sl 1, work 10 (10, 12, 12) sts in eye of partridge st, ssk, turn. Rep rows 2 and 3 until all sts are worked into heel turning—12 (12, 14, 14) sts. **Next rnd** With heel needle sts, pick up and k16 (17, 18, 19) sts along side (rows) of heel flap (*Needle 1*); pick up and k 32 (34, 36, 38) sts along side of mitered square and divide onto *Needles 2* and *3*, pick up and k 16 (17, 18, 19) sts along side (rows) of heel flap, k first half of heel sts with same needle (*Needle 4*)—a total of 76 (80, 86, 90) sts. Join and work in rnds. Pm at center back of heel to mark beg of rnd and sl marker every rnd.

Shape instep

Rnd 1 *Needle 1* K to last 3 sts, k2tog, k1; *Needle 2* and *3* knit; *Needle 4* k1, ssk, k to end. **Rnd 2** Knit. Rep last 2 rnds until 64 (68, 72, 76) sts rem, end with rnd 2.

LEG

Note Leg will be composed of 8 small mitered squares, worked separately and joined while working. With A, beg with the first st of the rnd, cast on 17 (18, 19, 20) sts at beg of rnd, then k these sts plus the 16 (17, 18, 19) sts on first needle for row 1 of mitered square and a total of 33 (35, 37, 39) sts. Leave rem sts on rnd unworked. Place removable marker at center st. **Row 2 (WS)** With A, k to center st, p1, k to end. **Row 3** With B, k to 1 st before center st, s2kp, k to end. **Row 4** With B, purl. Work these 4 rows foll chart 2 until 1 st rem. Leaving this st on needle, with color A and RS facing, pick up and k 17 (18, 19, 20) sts down the side of the mitered square just worked, then k16 (17, 18, 19) sts from next instep sts of rnd—33 (35, 37, 39) sts for mitered square. Work as for previous small mitered square. Work 2 more mitered squares as before ONLY join the 4th mitered square to the end of the first mitered square using RS join. Then cont to work 4 more mitered squares across tops of these squares to complete cuff. Cut B.

TOP RIBBING

With last A lp on needle, pick up and k sts for a total of 64 (68, 72, 76) sts around or 16 (17, 18, 19) sts on each of 4 needles. Join and work in rnds of k2, p2 rib for 1½"/4cm. Bind off loosely in rib.

FINISHING

Block socks, being careful not to flatten rib.

CHART 2

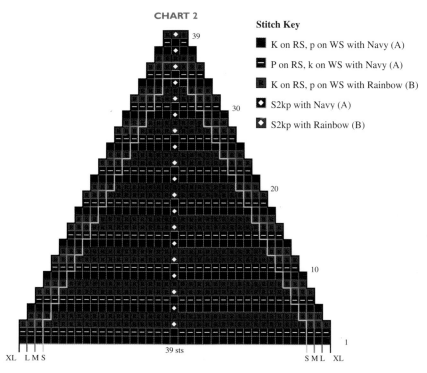

39 sts

XL L M S   S M L XL

Stitch Key

■ K on RS, p on WS with Navy (A)

▬ P on RS, k on WS with Navy (A)

▨ K on RS, p on WS with Rainbow (B)

◆ S2kp with Navy (A)

◇ S2kp with Rainbow (B)

CHART I

Stitch Key

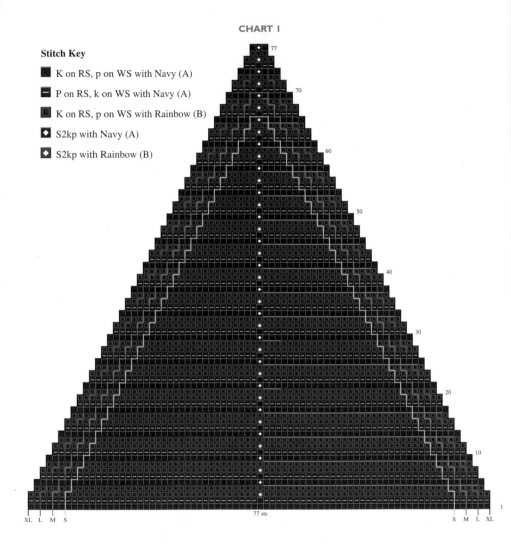

- K on RS, p on WS with Navy (A)
- P on RS, k on WS with Navy (A)
- K on RS, p on WS with Rainbow (B)
- S2kp with Navy (A)
- S2kp with Rainbow (B)

LAVENDER LACE SOCKS

Refined elegance

Traditional horseshoe lace pattern is worked along the leg and instep of this lovely Woman's sock. Designed by Evelyn Clark, reinforced heel and self-lace trim on the cuff make a stylish finish.

SIZE

Instructions are written for Woman's size Medium.

KNITTED MEASUREMENTS

- Leg width 7¼"/18.5cm
- Foot length 8½"/21.5cm

MATERIALS

- 2 1¾oz/50g balls (each approx 207yd/191m) of Lang/Berroco, Inc., *Jawoll Superwash* (wool ①) in #0107 lilac
- One set (5) size 0 (2mm) double pointed needles (dpn) *or size to obtain gauge*

GAUGE

40 sts and 54 rows/rnds to 4"/10cm over St st using size 0 (2mm) dpn.
Take time to check gauge.

NOTE

Heel is knit with a reinforcing strand of yarn, that is with 1 strand from outside and 1 strand from inside of same ball.

LACE PATTERN STITCH

(multiple of 9 sts)
Rnd 1 *P1, k7, p1; rep from * around.

Rnd 2 *P1, yo, k2, SK2P, k2, yo, p1; rep from * around.
Rnds 3 and 5 Rep rnd 1.
Rnd 4 *P1, k1, yo, k1, SK2P, k1, yo, k1, p1; rep from * around.
Rnd 6 *P1, k2, yo, SK2P, yo, k2, p1; rep from * around.
Rep rnds 1-6 for lace pat st.

CUFF

Using one needle, loosely cast on 72 sts. Divide sts on 4 needles with 18 sts on each needle. Join, taking care not to twist sts on needles. Mark end of rnd and sl marker every rnd. P 1 rnd. Beg with rnd 1, work in lace pat st, working 9-st rep 8 times around, until piece measures 7½"/19cm from beg, end with rnd 6, stretching slightly (or trying on to fit).

HEEL

Turn work. Sl 1, p35 heel sts. Leave rem 36 sts on 2 needles to be worked later for instep.
Row 2 (RS) Add another strand of yarn (reinforcing yarn) and *sl 1, k1; rep from * to end.
Row 3 Sl 1, p35.
Rep rows 2 and 3 until heel measures 2¼"/6cm, end with a RS row.

TURN HEEL

Row 1 Sl 1, p20, p2tog, p1, turn.
Row 2 Sl 1, k7, ssk, k1, turn.
Row 3 Sl 1, p8, p2tog, p1, turn.

Row 4 Sl 1, k9, ssk, k1, turn.
Row 5 Sl 1, p10, p2tog, p1, turn.
Row 6 Sl 1, k11, ssk, k1, turn.
Row 7 Sl 1, p12, p2tog, p1, turn.
Row 8 Sl 1, k13, ssk, k1, turn.
Row 9 Sl 1, p14, p2tog, p1, turn.
Row 10 Sl 1, k15, ssk, k1, turn.
Row 11 Sl 1, p16, p2tog, p1, turn.
Row 12 Sl 1, k17, ssk, k1, turn.
Row 13 Sl 1, p18, p2tog, p1, turn.
Row 14 Sl 1, k19, ssk, k1—22 sts. Cut reinforcing yarn.

With first needle, pick up and k18 sts along side (rows) of heel (*Needle 1*); [p1, k7, p1] twice (*Needle 2*); [p1, k7, p1] twice (*Needle 3*); pick up and k18 sts along side (rows) of heel and k11 sts from *Needle 1*, sl rem 11 sts onto first needle—there are 29 sts on first and fourth needles and 18 sts on 2nd and 3rd needles and a total of 94 sts.

SHAPE INSTEP

Rnd 1 *Needle 1* K11, [k1 tbl] 15 times, k2tog, k1 tbl; *Needles 2 and 3* work even in lace pat st; *Needle 4* k1 tbl, ssk, [k1tbl] 15 times, k11. **Rnd 2** *Needle 1* Knit; *Needles 2 and 3* work even in lace pat st;

Needle 4 knit. **Rnd 3** *Needle 1* K to last 3 sts, k2tog, k1; Needles 2 and 3 work even in lace pat st; *Needle 4* k1, ssk, k to end.
Rnd 4 Rep rnd 2. Rep rnd 3 and 4 until 72 sts rem and there are 18 sts on each needle. Work even as established until foot measures 7"/18cm from back of heel or 1½"/4cm less then desired length of foot (try on sock to ensure the correct length).

SHAPE TOE

Rnd 1 Knit.
Rnd 2 *Needle 1* K to last 3 sts, k2tog, k1; *Needle 2* k1, ssk, k to end; *Needle 3* k to last 3 sts, k2tog, k1; *Needle 4* k1, ssk, k to end.
Rnd 3 Knit.
Rep rnds 2 and 3 eight times more—36 sts rem. Then rep rnd 2 four times more—20 sts rem. Reposition sts as necessary on last rnd: *Needle 1* K3, k2tog, k1; *Needle 2* k1, ssk, k3 sts from *Needle 3*, k2tog, k1; *Needle 3* k1, ssk, k3, k4 from *Needle 1*—16 sts rem. Divide sts evenly onto 2 needles and weave toe sts tog using Kitchener st.

FINISHING

Block socks stretching slightly lengthwise.

TWO-NEEDLE SOCKS
Flat-out fantastic

Easy ribbing knit in a single strip then seamed is an ingenious way to create a classic sock style. Contrast color seaming paired with two different needle sizes make this unique design by Donna Druchunas.

SIZES

Instructions are written for Woman's size Medium. Changes for size Large in parentheses.

KNITTED MEASUREMENTS
- Leg width 7½"/19cm
- Foot length 8 (9)"/20.5 (23)cm

MATERIALS
- 2 1¾ oz/50g balls (each approx 137yd/126m) of Classic Elite Yarns *Waterspun* (wool ④) in #2546 aqua (A),
- Small amounts in #2515 teal (B)
- One pair each sizes 1 and 4 (2.25 and 3.5mm) needles *or size to obtain gauge*
- Size E/4 (3.5mm) crochet hook
- Tapestry needle

GAUGE

28 sts and 28 rows to 4"/10cm over k1, p1 rib using larger needles.
Take time to check gauge.

SOCKS

Beg at cuff edge with larger needles and A, cast on 25 sts.

Row 1 (RS) K1, [k1, p1] 11 times, k2.
Row 2 K1, [p1, k1] 12 times.
Rep these 2 rows for k1, p1 rib for 10 (12)"/25.5 (30.5)cm. This forms the leg and instep.

Shape toe

Change to smaller needle. Place yarn markers for toe after the first st and before the last st, inserting scrap yarn from back to front between the sts on each end of row. Work even for 2½"/6.5cm.

SOLE

Change to larger needles. Place yarn markers for the sole after the first st and before the last st, inserting scrap yarn from front to back between the sts on each end of row (figure 1). Work even for 5 (6)"/12.5 (15cm) from last markers.

Shape heel

Change to smaller needles. Place yarn markers for the heel after the first st and before the last st, inserting scrap yarn from back to front between the sts on each end of row. Work even for 2½"/6.5cm from last markers.

Back leg

Change to larger needles. Place yarn marker for the back leg after the first st and before the last st, inserting scrap yarn from front to back between the sts on each end of row. Work even for 5 (6)"/12.5 (15cm from last markers. Total length is 25 (29)"/63.5 (73.5)cm. Bind off loosely in rib.

With WS tog, tie the two ends of each set of markers as shown (figure 2).

Leg seams

Beg at the top of the leg seam with RS facing, stitch tog with B, making sure that the seam is loose enough to stretch with the rest of the knitting as foll: insert needle from the back to the front of the first garter-st ridge on the right piece, insert the needle from front to back on the first garter-st ridge on the left piece then from back to front on the 2nd ridge on right piece. Cont to work in this way inserting from front to back on the left piece and back to front on the right piece up to the heel marker. Cont to stitch past the heel marker (leaving the sts tied off by the marker for heel seam—figure 3). Cont stitching to the toe marker, remove marker and cont stitching until the seam is completely closed. Leave a 10"/26cm tail on the outside.

Heel seam

Remove heel marker. Beg at the left seam, work to the end of heel seam stitching as before. When closed, leave a 10"/26cm tail on the outside. Work other heel seam in same way.

Reinforcing heel and toe

Using the tail, weave across the toe seam 3 times. Reinforce heel in same way.

CROCHET EDGING

With crochet hook and B, sl st into first joining st at top of sock, *skip 1 purl st, ch 3, sl st into next k st; rep from * around, end with a sl st into first sl st. Fasten off. Wash and block socks flat to dry.

2

3

Breaking up

A medley of earthtone striping gives these socks their distinction. For easier working, the cuff and leg are knit flat on straight needles with the foot knit circularly on double pointed needles. Designed by Gayle Bunn.

SIZES
Instructions are written for Man's size Small/ Medium or Woman's size Large.

KNITTED MEASUREMENTS
- Leg width 8¾"/22cm
- Foot length 9½"/24cm

MATERIALS
- 1   1¼ oz/50g ball (each approx 223yd/204m) of Patons *Classic Merino Wool* (wool ④) each in #221 forest green (MC), #227 dk taupe (A), #229 lt taupe (B), #205 olive (C), #226 black (D), #206 rust (E), #208 burgundy (F) and #239 gold (G)
- One pair size 6 (4mm) needles *or size to obtain gauge*
- One set (4) size 6 (4mm) double pointed needles (dpn)
- Stitch holder

GAUGE
22 sts and 28 rows/rnds to 4"/10cm over St st using size 6 (4mm) needles.
Take time to check gauge.

Note When changing colors, twist yarns on WS to prevent holes.

LEFT SOCK
CUFF
With MC and straight needles, cast on 48 sts. **Row 1 (RS)** *K2, p2; rep from * to end. Work in k2, p2 rib as established for 3½"/9cm.
Beg leg chart
Next row (RS) Knit, foll row 1 of chart. Cont in St st and color pat foll leg chart through row 50. Change to dpn.

HEEL
Sl last 12 sts of row onto one dpn, then first 12 sts of row onto same needle—24 heel sts. Sl rem 24 sts to a st holder for instep. **Row 1 (RS)** With MC, *sl 1, k1; rep from * to end. **Row 2** Sl 1, p to end. Rep last 2 rows until heel measures 2¼"/6cm, end with a RS row.

Turn heel
Row 1 (WS) P15, p2tog, p1, turn.
Row 2 Sl 1, k7, SKP, k1, turn.
Row 3 Sl 1, p8, p2tog, p1, turn.
Row 4 Sl 1, k9, SKP, k1, turn.
Row 5 Sl 1, p10, p2tog, p1, turn.
Row 6 Sl 1, k11, SKP, k1, turn.
Row 7 Sl 1, p12, p2tog, p1, turn.
Row 8 Sl 1, k13, SKP, k1—16 sts. Cut MC.

Next rnd (RS) With MC, pick up and k 11 sts along left side (rows) of heel (*Needle 1*); k 24 sts of instep (*Needle 2*); pick up and k 11 sts along right side of heel, k 8 sts from heel onto end of needle (*Needle 3*); sl rem 8 heel sts onto end of Needle 1—62 total sts.

SHAPE INSTEP

Rnd 1 *Needle 1* k to last 3 sts, k2tog, k1; *Needle 2* knit; *Needle 3* k1, ssk, knit to end.

Rnd 2 With E, knit.

Rnd 3 With E, rep rnd 1.

Rnd 4 With MC, knit

Rnd 5 With MC, rep rnd 1.

Rnd 6 With E, knit.

Rnd 7 With E, rep rnd 1.

Rnd 8 With A, knit.

Rnd 9 With A, rep rnd 1.

Rnd 10 With C, knit.

Rnd 11 With C, rep rnd 1.

Rnd 12 With A, knit.

Rnd 13 With A, rep rnd 1—48 sts. Beg with rnd 15, work in stripe pat foll foot chart and cont through rnd 50 of chart.

SHAPE TOE

Cont with MC only, work as foll: **Rnd 1** *Needle 1* k to last 3 sts, k2tog, k1; *Needle 2* k1, ssk, k to last 3 sts, k2tog, k1; *Needle 3* k1, ssk, k to end of *Needle 3*. **Rnd 2** Knit. Rep last 2 rnds 5 times more—24 sts. Divide sts evenly onto 2 needles and weave toe sts tog using Kitchener st.

RIGHT SOCK

Work as for left sock, reversing placement of patchwork square on leg chart.

FINISHING

Block socks being careful not to flatten rib. Sew leg seam, sewing last half of rib from RS for cuff turnback.

FOOT

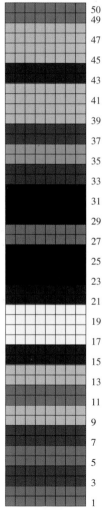

LEG

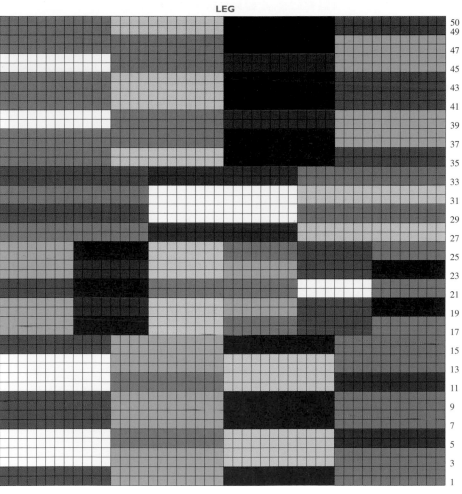

50
49
47
45
43
41
39
37
35
33
31
29
27
25
23
21
19
17
15
13
11
9
7
5
3
1

Color Key

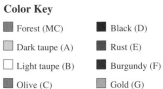

- Forest (MC)
- Dark taupe (A)
- Light taupe (B)
- Olive (C)
- Black (D)
- Rust (E)
- Burgundy (F)
- Gold (G)

GIRL'S ANKLET SOCKS
Tickled pink

Classic sock styling in a lightweight wool provides a wardrobe basic for the lucky little girl. Designed by Mary Saunders.

SIZES

Instructions are written for girl's size Small (5-6½). Changes for size Medium (6-7½) are in parentheses.

KNITTED MEASUREMENTS

- Leg width 6"/15cm
- Foot Length 6 (7)"/15 (18)cm

MATERIALS

- 1 1¾ oz/50g ball (each approx 184yd/170m) of GGH/Muench Yarns *Merino Soft* (wool ①) in #64 peach
- 1 set (5) size 1 (2.25mm) double point-ed needles (dpn) *or size to obtain gauge*
- Stitch holder

GAUGE

32 sts and 42 rows/rnds to 4"/10cm over St st using size 1 (2.25mm) dpn.
Take time to check gauge.

CUFF

Using one needle, cast on 56 sts. Divide sts on 4 needles with 14 sts on each nee-dle. Join, taking care not to twist sts on needles. Mark end of rnd and sl marker every rnd.

Foundation rnd *K1, p1; rep from * around.

Beg lace pat
Rnd 1 *K1, yo, [p1, k1] twice, p1, SK2P, [p1, k1] twice, p1, yo; rep from * around.
Rnd 2 *K2, [p1, k1] 6 times; rep from * around.
Rnd 3 *K1, yo, [k1, p1] twice, k1, SK2P, [k1, p1] twice, k1, yo; rep from * around.
Rnd 4 *K1, p1; rep from * around. Work rnds 1-4 once more.
Next rnd [K5, k2tog] 8 times—48 sts.
Cont in St st (k every rnd) until 2"/5cm are worked in St st.

HEEL

Next row With spare needle, k18, sl next 24 sts onto 2 needles for instep to be worked later. Turn and sl 1, p23—24 heel sts.
Row 1 *Sl 1, k1; rep from * to end.
Row 2 Sl 1, p23.
Rep these 2 rows 11 times more (25 rows in heel).

TURN HEEL

Row 1 Sl 1, k13, ssk, k1, turn.
Row 2 Sl 1, p5, p2tog, p1, turn.
Row 3 Sl 1, k6, ssk, k1, turn.
Row 4 Sl 1, p7, p2tog, p1, turn.
Cont to work in this way until there are 14 sts in heel, ending with a purl row (the last 2 rows will have the last 2 sts of row dec'd).

SHAPE INSTEP

Next rnd *Needle 1* K14 heel sts, pick up and k12 sts along side (rows) of heel (*Needle 1*); *Needle 2* k24 sts of instep; *Needle 3* pick up and k 12 sts along side (rows) of heel, k7 sts from *Needle 1*—62 sts.

Rnd 1 *Needle 1* K to last 3 sts, k2tog, k1; *Needle 2* knit; *Needle 3* k1, ssk, k to end.

Rnd 2 Knit.

Rep these 2 rnds 6 times more—48 sts rem. Cont in St st until foot measures 4½ (5½)"/11 (14)cm from back of heel or 1½"/4cm less than desired length of foot.

SHAPE TOE

Rnd 1 *Needle 1* K to last 3 sts, k2tog, k1; *Needle 2* k1, ssk, k to last 3 sts, k2tog, k1; *Needle 3* k1, ssk, k to end.

Rnd 2 Knit. Rep last 2 rows 6 times more—20 sts rem.

Then rep rnd 1 three times more—8 sts. Cut yarn leaving a 9"/23cm end. Draw yarn through rem sts and pull up tightly to secure.

FINISHING

Block socks being careful not to flatten.

Designer Lois S. Young works all the classic sock-making techniques. Alternating diamond cable patterns run along the leg and instep of this stylish woman's sock.

SIZE
Instructions are written for Woman's size Medium.

KNITTED MEASUREMENTS
- Leg width 8¼"/21cm
- Foot length 8½"/21.5cm

MATERIALS
- 3 1¾ oz/50g balls (each approx 136yd/125m) of Filatura Di Crosa/Tahki•Stacy Charles, Inc. *501* (wool ③) in #207 rust
- 1 set (5) size 3 (3mm) double pointed needles (dpn) *or size to obtain gauge*
- Cable needle
- Stitch markers

GAUGE
31 sts and 36 rnds to 4"/10cm over cable pat foll chart using size 3 (3mm) dpn.
Take time to check gauge.

STITCH GLOSSARY
1/1 RPC Sl 1 st to cn and hold to *back*, k1, then p1 from cn.
1/1 LPC Sl 1 st to cn and hold to *front*, p1, then k1 from cn.

C2R Sl 1 st to cn and hold to *back*, k1, then k1 from cn.
C2L Sl 1 st to cn and hold to *front*, k1, then k1 from cn.
SSP Sl 2 sts knitwise one at a time, return these 2 sts to LH needle and p2tog tbl.

BABY CABLE RIBBING
(multiple of 4 sts)
Rnd 1 *C2L, p2; rep from * around.
Rnd 2 *K2, p2; rep from * around.
Rep these 2 rnds for baby cable ribbing.

CUFF
Using one needle, cast on 64 sts. Divide sts on 4 needles with 16 sts on each needle. Join, taking care not to twist sts on needles. Mark end of rnd and sl marker every rnd. Work baby cable rib for 12 rnds, then work rnd 1 once more. On last rnd, remove rnd marker, sl 1 st and place new rnd marker (rnd is now positioned 1 st to the left to line up with the cable pat chart). Work rnd 1 of cable pat chart working 16-st rep 4 times and repositioning by one st on each needle, so that a complete rep is on each of the 4 needles. Cont to foll chart through rnd 16, then rep rnds 1-16 once, rnds 1-8 once.

HEEL
With spare needle, beg at right edge of heel, k2, p1, then sl the 27 sts from end of rnd to other end of same needle for heel, divide rem 34 sts onto 2 needles to be

worked later for instep. **Next row (WS)** Sl 1, k1, p26, k2. **Next row (RS)** Sl 1, k29. Rep these 2 rows until there are 31 rows in heel.

TURN HEEL

Row I (RS) Sl 1, k14, ssk, k1, turn.
Row 2 Sl 1, p1, p2tog, p1, turn.
Row 3 Sl 1, k3, ssk, k1, turn.
Row 4 Sl 1, p5, p2tog, p1, turn.
Row 5 Sl 1, k7, ssk, k1, turn.
Row 6 Sl 1, p9, p2tog, p1, turn.
Row 7 Sl 1, k11, ssk, k1, turn.
Row 8 Sl 1, p13, p2tog, p1, turn.
Row 9 Sl 1, k15, ssk, k1, turn.
Row 10 Sl 1, p17, p2tog, p1, turn—20 sts.
With spare needle, k20, pick up and k 16 sts along side (rows) of heel, p1, (*Needle 3*), pm for beg of rnd, cont 32 sts in cable pat as established (*Needle 1*), p1, pick up and k 16 sts along side (rows) of heel—86 sts. K all sts around to 2 sts before beg of rnd.

SHAPE INSTEP

*Ssp, work 32 sts of *Needle 1*, p2tog, k until 2 sts before beg of rnd (2 sts dec'd). Rep from * 10 times more—64 sts. Reposition sts so that there are 16 sts on *Needles 2 and 3* and 32 sts on *Needle 1* and cont in pats as established until there are a total of five 16-rnd reps along instep from beg of sock. Work rnds 1-8 once, foot measures 6½"/16.5cm from back of heel.

SHAPE TOE

Rnd I *Needle 1* K1, ssk, k to last 3 sts, k2tog, k1; *Needle 2* k1, ssk, k to end; *Needle 3* k to last 3 sts, k2tog, k1. **Rnd 2** Knit.
Rep last 2 rnds 8 times more—28 sts rem. Divide sts evenly onto 2 needles and weave toe sts tog using Kitchener st.

FINISHING

Block socks being careful not to flatten rib.

CABLE PATTERN

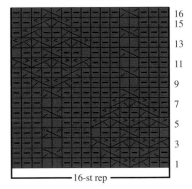

16
15
13
11
9
7
5
3
1

— 16-st rep —

Stitch Key

☐ K on RS, p on WS

⊟ P on RS, k on WS

1/1 RPC

1/1 LPC

C2R

C2L

STRIPED SHEEP SOCKS

Mad about ewe

Variegated stripes form the handsome background for these thick wool socks, while duplicate-stitch sheep decorate the cuffs. Designed by Gitta Schrade for men or women.

SIZE
Instructions are written for Woman's size X-Large or Man's size Medium.

KNITTED MEASUREMENTS
■ Leg width 8¾"/22cm
■ Foot length 10"/25.5cm

MATERIALS
Note All yarns are Naturally/S.R. Kertzer

■ 1 3½ oz/100g skein (each approx 183yd/167m) of *Aspiring 10-Ply* (wool/alpaca ④) in #705 black (A)
■ 1 3½ oz/100g skein each (each approx 175yd/160m) of *Tussock 10-ply* (wool/polyester ④) in #170 orange (B) and #168 grey (C)
■ 1 3½ oz/100g skein (each approx 180yd/167m) of *Aran 10-Ply* (wool ④) in #321 natural (D)
■ 1 1¾ oz/50g ball (each approx 83yd/77m) of *Café* (wool/alpaca/mohair/nylon ④) in #710 cream (E)
■ 1 set (5) each sizes 6 and 7 (4 and 4.5mm) double pointed needles (dpn) *or size to obtain gauge*
■ Stitch markers

GAUGE
22 sts and 30 rows/rnds to 4"/10cm over St st using larger dpn.
Take time to check gauge.

Note Sheep are embroidered foll chart using duplicate st after the socks are knit.

CUFF
Using one smaller needle, with A, cast on 48 sts. Divide sts on 3 needles with 16 sts on each needle. Join, taking care not to twist sts on needles. Mark end of rnd and sl marker every rnd. Working in k2, p2 rib, work 1 rnd with A, 4 rnds with B, 3 rnds with A, 3 rnds with B. Change to larger dpn. Then cont in St st (k every rnd) with B for 20 rnds. **Next rnd** *K2 with D, k2 with A; rep from * around. Rep this rnd once more. Then work 2 rnds C, 2 rnds B, 2 rnds A and 2 rnds D.

HEEL
Sl last 12 sts from needle 3 onto spare needle, then sl first 12 sts from *Needle 1* onto other end of same needle—24 heel sts. Divide rem 24 sts onto 2 needles to be worked later for instep. Work on 24 heel sts with B back and forth in rows. **Row 1 (WS)** With B, sl 1, p to end. **Row 2** *Sl 1, k1; rep from * to end. Rep these 2 rows until there are 17 rows in heel.

TURN HEEL
Row 1 K14, ssk, k1, turn.

Row 2 Sl 1, p5, p2tog, p1, turn.
Row 3 Sl 1, k6, ssk, k1, turn.
Row 4 Sl 1, p7, p2tog, p1, turn.

Cont to work heel shaping in this way, working 1 more st between dec's each row until all sts are worked—14 sts.

Next rnd (RS) With A, sl first 7 sts onto spare needle. With another spare needle, k7 (the rem heel sts) then with same needle, pick up and k 12 sts along side (rows) of heel, (*Needle 1*), pm; with *Needle 2*, k24 sts of instep, pm; with *Needle 3*, pick up and k12 sts along side (rows) of heel, k7 rem heel sts—62 sts.

SHAPE INSTEP

Rnd I K to 2 sts before first marker, k2tog, k to 2nd marker, sl marker and ssk, k to end. K 1 rnd. Rep last 2 rnds 6 times more, AT SAME TIME, work stripes working a total of 4 rnds with A (including pick-up rnd), 2 rnds D, 3 rnds A, then cont with C for 6 rnds—48 sts after instep shaping is completed. Then cont stripe pat, with 4 rnds more with C, 2 rnds A, 14 rnds B, 2 rnds A, 3 rnds D, then cont with B for 8 rnds or until foot measures 8"/20.5cm from back of heel or 2"/5cm less than desired length of foot.

SHAPE TOE

Cont with A only and divide sts on 3 needles as foll: 12 sts on *Needle 1*, 24 sts on *Needle 2*, 12 sts on *Needle 1*.

Rnd I *Needle 1* K to last 3 sts, k2tog, k1; *Needle 2* k1, ssk, k to last 3 sts, k2tog, k1; *Needle 3* k1, ssk, k to end. **Rnd 2** Knit.

Rep last 2 rnds 5 times more—24 sts rem. Divide sts evenly onto 2 needles and weave toe sts tog using Kitchener st.

FINISHING

Centering sheep chart on one side of cuff section in A, embroider sheep foll chart using duplicate st. Work another sheep on opposite side of cuff. Work other sock in same way. Block socks being careful not to flatten rib.

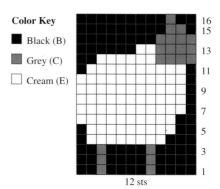

Color Key

■ Black (B)

■ Grey (C)

☐ Cream (E)

16
15
13
11
9
7
5
3
1

12 sts

Mari Lynn Patrick's ballet-style slippers make for a perfect fit. They feature clever detailing such as short row shaping on the heels, garter stitch soles and single crochet finishing worked over elastic thread.

SIZES

Instructions are written for Woman's size Small (6½-7). Changes for sizes Medium (7½-8), Large (8½-9) and X-Large (9½-10) are in parentheses. All sizes are for shoe sizes, not sock sizes.

MATERIALS

- 2 1¾ oz/50g skeins (each approx 107yd/98m) of Lion Brand *AL•PA•KA* (acrylic/alpaca/wool ⑤) in #149 lt grey (A)
- 1 skein in #249 dk grey (B)
- 1 set (5) size 7 (4.5mm) double pointed needles (dpn) or size to obtain gauge
- Size G/6 (4.5mm) crochet hook
- 1 yd/1m black oval elastic
- Dk grey thread
- Stitch markers

GAUGES

- 14 sts and 28 rows to 4"/10cm over garter st using double strand of yarn and size 7 (4.5mm) needles.
- 14 sts and 24 rows to 4"/10cm over St st using double strand of yarn and size 7 (4.5mm) needles.

Take time to check gauges.

W & T
Wrap and turn (see page 14 for details).

Note Work with 2 strands of yarn held tog throughout.

RIGHT SOLE

With 2 strands of B, cast on 4 sts. Using 2 dpn and working back and forth in rows, work in garter st as foll:

Row 1 (RS) K2, inc 1 st in next st, k1.
Row 2 K3, inc 1 st in next st, k1.
Row 3 K4, inc 1 st in next st, k1.
Row 4 K5, inc 1 st in next st, k1—8 sts.
K14 (12, 12, 10) rows.
Next row K to last 3 sts, k2tog, k1. K 9 (7, 7, 7) rows.
Next row K1, inc 1 st in next st, k to last 2 sts, inc 1 st in next st, k1. Place yarn markers each side of this row. K9 (9, 7, 5) rows.
Next row K to last 2 sts, inc 1 st in next st, k1. K 5 (5, 3, 3) rows.
Next row K to last 2 sts, inc 1 st in next st, k1. K9 (7, 7, 7) rows.
*****Next row** K1, k2tog, k to last 3 sts, k2tog, k1*. K5 (5, 5, 3) rows. Rep between *'s once. K5 (5, 3, 3) rows. Rep between *'s once. K 1 row. Bind off 5 sts.

LEFT SOLE

Work as for right sole (pattern is reversible).

SLIPPER SIDES

Note Sides of slipper are picked up on 4

dpn and worked in rnds. To space picking up sts evenly, pick up and k 1 st in between each ridge 4 times, then pick up 1 st in garter ridge (for approx 5 sts picked up every 10 rows). With 2 strands A, beg at center toe st, pick up and k 3 sts across toe, 16 (19, 22, 24) sts to marker (for *Needle 1*); 15 (16, 17, 19) sts to center back heel (for *Needle 2*), 15 (16, 17, 19) sts to 2nd marker (for *Needle 3*), 15 (18, 21, 23) sts to end (for *Needle 4*)—64 (72, 80, 88) sts. Join and work in rnds. K 1 rnd.

Beg short-row heel shaping

Next rnd K to end of *Needle 2*, k5 on *Needle 3*, w & t.

Next row P10, w & t.

Next row K13, w & t.

Next row P16, w & t. **Next row** K all sts to end of rnd.

K 4 rnds more. Cut yarn. Slide last 10 sts of *Needle 4* to beg of *Needle 1*. Rejoin yarn to new sts on *Needle 1*.

TOE SHAPING

Working across next 21 sts, k2tog while binding off these 21 sts, k to end of rnd. Turn.

Next row Bind off 5 sts, p to end. **Next row** Bind off 5 sts, k to end.

Next row Bind off 7 (7, 8, 9) sts, p to end.

Next row Bind off 7 (7, 8, 9) sts, k to end. Bind off rem sts.

INSTEP

With 2 strands of A, cast on 8 sts. Using 2 dpn and working back and forth in rows, work in St st for 16 rows. Dec 1 st at beg of next 4 rows. Bind off 4 sts.

FINISHING

Place instep at toe edge of slipper, centering evenly. Pm or baste in place. With 2 strands A, whip st instep to slipper.

TRIM

With crochet hook and 2 strands B, work sc evenly across 8 instep sts, then cont to work over elastic, work sc evenly around slipper top and join to instep, pulling up elastic for a snug fit. Knot elastic at both ends and secure.

LOOP

With crochet hook and 2 strands B, ch 20. Place ch at 1¼"/3cm above instep and make a loop at center. Sew neatly in place with thread.

TEXTURED FAIR ISLE SOCKS

Pitter pattern

An easy **Fair Isle** pattern lends charm to **Gayle Bunn's** wool socks. In shades of blue and green, a striking palette creates a dramatic effect.

SIZE

Instructions are written for Man's size Small/ Medium or Woman's size Large.

KNITTED MEASUREMENTS

- Leg width 9½"/24cm
- Foot length 10"/25.5cm

MATERIALS

- 2 1¾oz/50g balls (each approx 128yd/ 117m) of Patons® *Country Garden DK* (wool ②) in #71 navy (MC)
- 1 ball each in #37 dk green (A), #58 lt blue (B), #79 denim blue (C), and #38 lt green (D)
- One set (4) size 5 (3.75mm) double pointed needles (dpn) *or size to obtain gauge*
- Stitch holder

GAUGE

25 sts and 33 rows/rnds to 4"/10cm over St st foll chart using size 5 (3.75mm) needles.
Take time to check gauge.

Note When changing colors, twist yarns on WS to prevent holes. Purl sts on chart in background color are indicated with purl symbol (-).

CUFF

Beg at top edge, with MC cast on 60 sts. Divide sts on three needles with 20 sts on each needle. Join, taking care not to twist sts on needles. Mark end of rnd and sl marker every rnd. Work around in k1, p1 rib for 1½"/4cm. Then foll chart 1, work 10-st rep 6 times. Work through row 19 of chart 1. Then foll chart 2, work 6-st rep 10 times. Work through row 22 of chart 2.

HEEL

Sl last 15 sts of *Needle 3* and first 15 sts of *Needle 1* onto one dpn—30 heel sts. Sl rem 30 sts to a holder for instep.
Row 1 (RS) With MC, *sl 1, k1; rep from * to end.
Row 2 Sl 1, p to end.
Rep last 2 rows until heel measures 2¼"/6cm, end with a RS row.

TURN HEEL

Row 1 (WS) P17, p2tog, p1, turn.
Row 2 Sl 1, k5, SKP, k1, turn.
Row 3 Sl 1, p6, p2tog, p1, turn.
Row 4 Sl 1, k7, SKP, k1, turn.
Row 5 Sl 1, p8, p2tog, p1, turn.
Row 6 Sl 1, k9, SKP, k1, turn.
Row 7 Sl 1, p10, p2tog, p1, turn.
Row 8 Sl 1, k11, SKP, k1, turn.
Row 9 Sl 1, p12, p2tog, p1, turn.
Row 10 Sl 1, k13, SKP, k1.
Row 11 Sl 1, p14, p2tog, p1, turn.
Row 12 Sl 1, k15, SKP, k1—18 sts. Cut yarn.
Next rnd (RS) With A and spare needle, pick up and k 14 sts along left side (rows)

of heel (*Needle 1*); k30 sts of instep (*Needle 2*); pick up and k 14 sts along right side of heel, k9 sts from heel onto end of needle (*Needle 3*); sl rem 9 heel sts onto end of *Needle 1*—76 total sts. Rejoin yarn at beg of *Needle 1*.

SHAPE INSTEP

Rnd 1 *Needle 1* [K1, p1] 10 times, k2tog, p1; *Needle 2* [k1, p1] 15 times; *Needle 3* k1, ssk, [k1, p1] 10 times.
Rnd 2 *P1, k1; rep from * around.
Rnd 3 *Needle 1* K to last 3 sts, k2tog, k1; *Needle 2* knit; *Needle 3* k1, ssk, knit to end.
Rnd 4 Knit.
Beg with rnd 8 of chart 1, cont to foll chart 1 and shape instep working rnds 3 and 4

six times more—60 sts, AT SAME TIME, when chart 1 is completed, foll rows 1-22 of chart 2 once, then rows 3-19 of chart 1 once. **Next rnd** With MC, knit.

SHAPE TOE

Cont with MC only, work as foll:
Rnd 1 *Needle 1* K to last 3 sts, k2tog, k1; *Needle 2* k1, ssk, k to last 3 sts, k2tog, k1; *Needle 3* k1, ssk, knit to end of needle.
Rnd 2 Knit. Rep last 2 rnds 7 times more—28 sts. Divide sts evenly onto 2 needles and weave toe sts tog using Kitchener st.

FINISHING

Block socks being careful not to flatten rib.

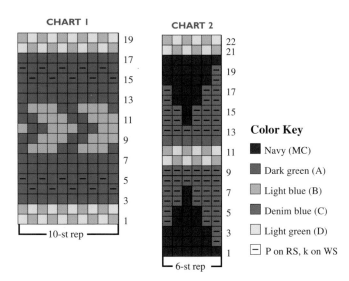

CHART I

19
17
15
13
11
9
7
5
3
1

— 10-st rep —

CHART 2

22
21
19
17
15
13
11
9
7
5
3
1

— 6-st rep —

Color Key

■ Navy (MC)
■ Dark green (A)
□ Light blue (B)
■ Denim blue (C)
□ Light green (D)
⊟ P on RS, k on WS

Red hot chili peppers

Variegated yarn along the instep works with a solid color yarn in ribs to give these socks sizzling appeal. Designed in shades of red by Veronica Manno.

SIZES

Instructions are written for Woman's size Medium.

KNITTED MEASUREMENTS

- Leg width 7½"/19cm
- Foot length 8"/20.5cm

MATERIALS

- 2 1¾ oz/50g hanks each (each approx 175yd/161m) of Koigu Wool Designs *Premium Merino* (wool ①) in #2227 red (A)
- 1 ball in #P621 red multi (B)
- One set (3) size 3 (3mm) double pointed needles (dpn) *or size to obtain gauge*

GAUGE

29 sts and 35 rows/rnds to 4"/10cm over St st using size 3 (3mm) dpn.
Take time to check gauge.

CUFF

With A and one needle, cast on 20 sts, then cont with B cast on 14 sts, then with A, cast on 20 sts—54 sts. Divide sts on 3 needles with 20 sts on *Needle 1*, 14 sts on *Needle 2* and 20 sts on *Needle 3*. Join, taking care not to twist sts on needles. Mark end of rnd and sl marker every rnd.

Rnd 1 With A, [k3, p2] 4 times (*Needle 1*); with B, k14 (*Needle 2*); with A, [p2, k3] 4 times (*Needle 3*). Cont in rib and St st as established for 5"/12.5cm.

Separate at heel

Sl first 13 sts of *Needle 1* and last 13 sts of *Needle 3* to spare needle to be worked later for heel.

Instep

Cont in colors and pat as established, rib 7 rem sts from *Needle 1* with A, k14 with B, rib rem 7 sts with A—28 instep sts. Working back and forth in rows in established colors on instep sts only, work even for 5½"/14cm more. Leave sts on hold.

HEEL

Return to 26 heel sts and work even in rows of rib for 20 rows.

Turn heel

Row 1 (RS) K18, SKP, turn.
Row 2 Sl 1, p10, p2tog, turn.
Row 3 Sl 1, k10, SKP, turn.
Row 4 Rep row 2.
Rep last 2 rows until 12 sts rem, end with a p row. Cut yarn.

Shape instep

With spare needle and A, pick up and k 14 sts along right side of heel, k6 sts of heel on same needle, with another needle, k rem 6 heel sts, pick up and k 14 sts along left side of heel—40 sts.
Next row Purl.
Next row K1, SKP, k to last 3 sts, k2tog, k1.
Next row K1, p to last st, k1.
Rep last 2 rows until there are heel 28 sts.

FOOT

Work even in St st on these sts until there are same number of rows as instep.

Shape toe

Reposition sts beg at last 14 sts of foot (*Needle 1*), 28 sts of instep (*Needle 2*), rem 14 sts of foot (*Needle 3*). Rejoin yarn to work in rnds for toe with A only.

Rnd 1 Knit.

Rnd 2 *Needle 1* K to last 3 sts, k2tog, k1; *Needle 2* k1, SKP, k to last 3 sts, k2tog, k1; *Needle 3* k1, SKP, k to end. Rep these 2 rnds until 16 sts rem. Divide sts onto 2 needles and weave toe sts tog using Kitchener st.

FINISHING

Block socks, being careful not to flatten rib. Sew instep and foot seams.

BASIC RIBBED SOCKS

All in the family

Shape toe

Beg at center of sole, k to last 3 sts of *Needle 1*, k2tog, k1; on *Needle 2*, k1, ssk, k to last 3 sts, k2tog, k1; on *Needle 3*, k1, SSK, k to end. K 1 rnd. Rep last 2 rnds until 16 sts rem. K4 sts of *Needle 1*, sl on *Needle 3* (sole sts).

FINISHING

See Man's Finishing.

WOMAN'S SOCKS

CUFF

Cast on 66 sts loosely and divide on 3 needles. Join, taking care not to twist sts. Place marker for end of rnd and sl marker every rnd. Work in k1, p1 rib for 2"/5cm.

LEG

Rnd 1 K2, *p2, k4; rep from * around. Rep rnd 1 for pat until piece measures 3"/7.5cm from beg of leg. Work next 32 sts to 2 needles for instep, k rem 34 sts on one needle for heel, dec 2 sts evenly spaced across heel sts—32 heel sts.

HEEL

Row 1 (WS) Sl 1 purlwise, p to end.
Row 2 *Wyib sl 1 purlwise, k1; rep from * to end.
Rep last 2 rows 14 times more.

Turn heel

Next row (WS) Sl 1, p18, p2tog, p1, turn.
Next row Sl 1, k7, SSK, k1, turn.

Next row Sl 1, p8, p2tog, p1, turn.
Next row Sl 1, k9, SSK, k1, turn.
Next row Sl 1, p10, p2tog, p1, turn.
Cont to work toward sides of heel, having 1 st more before dec on each row, until 20 sts rem.

GUSSET AND FOOT

With same needle, pick up and k 16 sts on side edge of heel; with *Needle 2*, cont in pat on 32 instep sts; with *Needle 3*, pick up and k 16 sts on other side of heel, k10 heel sts to same needle. Place marker for end of rnd and center of sole (26 sts on each of *Needles 1 and 3*, 32 sts on 2nd, or instep needle). Work 1 rnd, in pat as established. **Next rnd** K to last 3 sts of end of *Needle 1*, k2tog, k1; on *Needle 2* work across instep sts; on *Needle 3*, k1, ssk, k to end. Rep last 2 rnds 9 times more—64 sts. Cont to work in pat on instep sts until 1¾"/4.5cm less than desired finished length (16 sts on each of *Needles 1 and 3*, 32 sts on 2nd or instep needle).

Shape toe

Beg at center of sole, k to last 3 sts of *Needle 1*, k2tog, k1; on *Needle 2*, k1, ssk, k to last 3 sts, k2tog, k1; on *Needle 3*, k1, ssk, k to end. K 1 rnd. Rep last 2 rnds until 16 sts rem. K4 sts of *Needle 1* and sl to *Needle 3*.

FINISHING

See Man's Finishing.

For Intermediate Knitters

Picot-turned top trim and a Fair Isle zig zag pattern lend whimsey to the cuff details on these socks. Designed by Petra Noyes in a lovely lightweight tweed wool.

SIZES

Instructions are written for Woman's size Small. Changes for sizes Medium and Large are in parentheses.

KNITTED MEASUREMENTS

- Leg width 8½ (9, 9½)"/21.5 (23, 24)cm
- Foot length 7 (8, 9)"/18 (20.5, 23)cm

MATERIALS

- 2 .88oz/25g skeins (each approx 160yd/ 148m) of Rowan Yarns *4-Ply Tweed* (wool ②) in #701 deep red (MC)
- 1 skein each in #705 orange (A), #710 burgundy (B), #704 slate (C) and #702 stone (D)
- One pair size 2 (2.75mm) needles *or size to obtain gauge*
- One set (5) size 2 (2.75mm) double pointed needles (dpn)
- Stitch markers

GAUGE

28 sts and 42 rows/rnds to 4"/10cm over St st using size 2 (2.75mm) needles.
Take time to check gauge.

Note Sock is worked back and forth in rows on straight needles to just before heel, then sts are divided onto dpn and worked in rnds.

CUFF

With straight needles and MC, cast on 72 sts. K 1 row, p 1 row. Change to C and work 4 rows in St st. **Next (picot) row** K1, *k2tog, yo; rep from * to end. P 1 row, k 1 row, p 1 row, k 1 row.

Beg chart pat

Next row Cont in St st, work 24-st rep of chart 3 times. Cont to foll chart through row 35. With MC, k next row dec 12 (8, 6) sts evenly spaced—60 (64, 66) sts. Cont with MC, work in St st for 19 rows more. Using dpn, k15 (16, 16) sts on *Needle 1*, 30 (32, 34) sts on *Needle 2* (instep), 15 (16, 16) sts on *Needle 3*. Join, taking care not to twist sts on needles. Mark end of rnd and sl marker every rnd. With MC, k 10 rnds.

HEEL

With spare needle, k15 (16, 16) sts from *Needle 1*, sl the 15 (16, 16) sts from *Needle 3* onto other end of needle for 30 (32, 32) heel sts. Divide rem 30 (32, 34) instep sts onto 2 needles to be worked later for instep. Work back and forth in rows on heel sts only for a total of 20 (22, 22) rows.

Turn heel

Row 1 (RS) K23 (24, 24), k2tog tbl, turn.
Row 2 Sl 1, p16; p2tog, turn.
Row 3 Sl 1, k16, k2tog tbl, turn.

Rep last 2 rows until all sts are worked and 18 heel sts rem.

Next rnd K9 sts and leave on needle, with spare needle, k9 rem heel sts, pick up and k15 (15, 16) sts along side edge (rows) of heel (*Needle 1*); work instep 30 (32, 34) sts (*Needle 2*); pick up and k15 (15, 16) sts along side edge (rows) of heel, k rem 9 heel sts (*Needle 3*)—a total of 78 (80, 84) sts.

Shape instep

Rnd 1 Knit.

Rnd 2 *Needle 1* K to last 2 sts, k2tog; *Needle 2* knit; *Needle 3* k2tog tbl, k to end. Rep last 2 rnds 8 (7, 8) times more—60 (64, 66) sts. Work even until foot measures 5 (6, 7)"/13 (15.5, 18)cm from back of heel, or 2"/5cm less than desired length of foot.

Shape toe

Rnd 1 *Needle 1* K to last 3 sts, k2tog, k1; *Needle 2* k1, k2tog tbl, k to last 3 sts, k2tog, k1; *Needle 3* k1, k2tog tbl, k to end.

Rnd 2 Knit. Rep these 2 rnds 7 (8, 8) times more—28 (28, 30) sts rem. Divide sts evenly onto 2 needles and weave toe sts tog using Kitchener st.

FINISHING

Block socks being careful not to flatten. Turn top hems at picot row and sew to WS. Sew back leg seam.

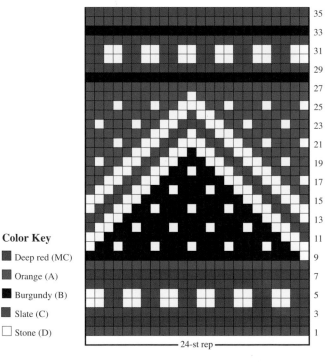

Color Key

■ Deep red (MC)

■ Orange (A)

■ Burgundy (B)

■ Slate (C)

□ Stone (D)

— 24-st rep —

35 33 31 29 27 25 23 21 19 17 15 13 11 9 7 5 3 1

CHILD'S BEE SLIPPERS
What's the buzz?

Slippers with bumblebee striping are sure to delight your little ones. This winsome treasure has true-to-life eyes, wings and antennaes and is felted for extra durability. Designed by Jean Guirguis.

SIZE

Instructions are written for Child's size Small (5-6½).

KNITTED MEASUREMENTS

- Leg width 5½"/14cm
- Foot length 5½"/14cm

MATERIALS

- 1 4oz/113g skein each (each approx 190yd/173m) of Brown Sheep Co., *Lamb's Pride Worsted* (wool ④) in #M-05 onyx (A) and #M-155 lemon (B)
- 1 set (4) size 7 (4.5mm) double pointed needles (dpn) *or size to obtain gauge*
- 4 plastic eyes (with shanks for sewing)
- 1 square black felt
- Fabric glue
- 2 black pipe cleaners
- Heavy sewing thread and needle

GAUGE

18 sts and 24 rows/rnds to 4"/10cm over St st (before felting) using size 7 (4.5mm) dpn. *Take time to check gauge.*

CUFF

Using one needle, with A, cast on 32 sts. Divide sts on 3 needles with 12 sts on *Needle 1*, 10 sts on *Needle 2* and 10 sts on *Needle 3*. Join, taking care not to twist sts on needles. Mark end of rnd and sl marker every rnd. Work in k1, p1 rib for 5"/12.5cm.

HEEL

With spare needle, sl first 16 sts on this needle (heel), sl rem 16 sts onto 2 needles to be worked later for instep.
Row 1 (RS) *K1, sl 1; rep from *, end k2.
Row 2 Purl. Rep these 2 rows until heel measures 2"/5cm, end with a RS row.

Turn heel
Row 1 (WS) P10, p2tog, p1, turn.
Row 2 Sl 1, k5, k2tog, k1, turn.
Row 3 Sl 1, p6, p2tog, p1, turn.
Row 4 Sl 1, k7, k2tog, k1, turn.
Row 5 Sl 1, p8, p2tog, turn.
Row 6 Sl 1, k8, k2tog—10 sts.

Shape instep
Using same needle with heel sts, pick up and k8 sts along side (rows) of heel (*Needle 1*); k16 instep sts (*Needle 2*), pick up and k8 sts along side (rows) of heel and k5 from *Needle 1* (*Needle 3*)—42 sts.
Rnd 1 *Needle 1* K to last 3 sts, k2tog, k1; *Needle 2* knit; *Needle 3* k1, k2tog, k to end. **Rnd 2** Knit. Rep last 2 rnds 4 times more—32 sts rem.

FOOT

[K 1 rnd with A, k 1 rnd B] 8 times, foot measures approx 5"/12.5cm from back of heel, or 2"/5cm less than desired length of foot. (This measurement is before felting which will cause length to shrink to knitted measurement).

Shape toe

Cont with A only.

Dec rnd *Needle 1* K to last 3 sts, k2tog, k1; *Needle 2* k1, k2tog, k to last 3 sts, k2tog, k1; *Needle 3* k1, k2tog, k to end. K 3 rnds. Rep dec rnd. K 2 rnds. Rep dec rnd. *K 1 rnd. Rep dec rnd*. Rep between *'s once—12 sts rem. Divide sts evenly onto 2 needles and weave toe sts tog using Kitchener st.

FINISHING

For felting process, first weave in loose ends then place slippers in washing machine with mild soapy detergent and set on hot. Add several towels to the wash cycle for extra abrasion. After cycle is finished, mold socks to shape while damp and place in dryer on hot setting for 10-20 minutes, checking often and molding into shape with hands as before. Remove before completely dry and stuff with yarn or cloth to dry to desired shape. Cut 8 felt wings for each slipper foll template. Glue 2 wings tog for each wing and sew with large stitch at top of striping (see photo). Sew on eyes. Draw pipe cleaner through as shown and bend at ends.

BEE WING TEMPLATE

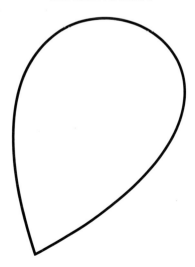

Non-traditional shades of baby pink and blue in a quick-to-knit pattern make the ideal baby gift. Boy's style sports a slanting cable pattern while girl's has lacy eyelets. Both designed by Lila Chin.

SIZES

Instructions are written for infant's size 3-6 months. Changes for sizes 9-12 months are in parentheses.

KNITTED MEASUREMENTS

■ Leg width 4½"/11.5cm
■ Foot length 3¼ (3¾)"/8 (9.5)cm

MATERIALS

■ 1 1¾oz/50g ball (each approx 187yd/170m) of Lane Borgosesia *Merinos Extra Fine* (wool ②) in #257 blue or #66 peach
■ One set (4) size 2 (2.75mm) double pointed needles (dpn) *or size to obtain gauge*
■ Stitch markers

GAUGE

28 sts and 40 rnds/rows to 4"/10cm over chart pat using size 2 (2.75mm) needle. *Take time to check gauge.*

CUFF

Beg at cuff edge, cast on 32 sts on one needle. Divide sts onto 3 needles, with 10 sts on *Needle 1*, 12 sts on *Needle 2* and 10 sts on *Needle 3*. Join, taking care not to twist sts on needles. Mark end of rnd and sl marker every rnd. Work in k2, p2 rib for 5 rnds. K 2 rnds. Then beg with rnd 1 of chart for chosen style, work 8-st rep 4 times. Work through rnd 10. Then work rnds 1-9 once.

HEEL

Rnd 10 Knit sts on *Needle 1*, knit sts on *Needle 2*, k first 2 sts of *Needle 3*, then sl the 2 sts just worked onto end of *Needle 2* and last 2 sts of *Needle 1* onto beg of *Needle 2*—16 instep sts. Divide these sts onto 2 needles and leave to be worked later for instep. Rejoin yarn to 8 sts of *Needle 3* and k these 8 sts, k8 sts of *Needle 1*—16 heels sts. Work back and forth in rows on the 16 heel sts only.

Row 1 (WS) Sl 1, p to end.
Row 2 Sl 1, *k1, sl 1; rep from *, end k1. Rep these 2 rows until heel measures ¾"/2cm, end with a RS row.

Turn heel
Next row (WS) P10, p2tog, p1, turn.
Row 2 Sl 1, k5, ssk, k1, turn.
Row 3 Sl 1, p6, p2tog, p1, turn.
Row 4 Sl 1, k7, ssk, k1, turn.
Row 5 Sl 1, p8, p2tog, p1, turn.
Row 6 Sl 1, k8, ssk—10 sts. Cut yarn. Sl last 5 sts of heel to spare needle and cont to pick up with same needle—8 sts from side of heel (13 sts on *Needle 1*); work 16 instep sts cont in chart pat, (*Needle 2*); pick up and k8 sts from other side of heel and k5 from first needle (13 sts on *Needle 3*) for a total of 42 sts.

Shape instep

Rnd 1 Knit.

Rnd 2 *Needle 1* K to last 3 sts, ssk, k1; *Needle 2* work even in chart pat; *Needle 3* k1, k2tog, k to end. Rep last 2 rnds 4 times more—32 sts. Then work even in chart pat on instep sts and St st on sole sts until foot measures 3¼ (3¾)"/8 (9.5)cm from beg of heel.

Shape toe

Rnd 1 *Needle 1* K to last 3 sts, ssk, k1; *Needle 2* k1, k2tog, k to last 3 sts, ssk, k1, *Needle 3* k1, k2tog, k to end.

Rnd 2 Knit. Rep last 2 rnds 3 times more—16 sts. Divide sts evenly onto 2 needles and weave toe sts tog using Kitchener st.

FINISHING

Block socks being careful not to flatten rib.

Girl Version Chart

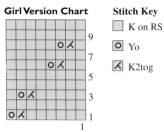

Stitch Key

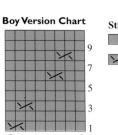
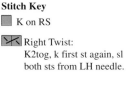

K on RS

Yo

K2tog

Boy Version Chart

Stitch Key

K on RS

Right Twist:
K2tog, k first st again, sl both sts from LH needle.

TEXTURED SOCKS
All that jazz

Very Easy Very Vogue

Designed by Norah Gaughan, these handsome socks marry two shades of heathered yarn to create subtle artful color play. Alternating the two colors for the foot, toes and heels plus a circular knit heel gives these socks a unique appeal.

SIZE

Instructions are written for Woman's size Medium/Large.

KNITTED MEASUREMENTS

■ Leg width 8"/20.5cm
■ Foot length 9"/23cm

MATERIALS

■ 1 5oz/150g skein (each approx 246yd/227m) of JCA Artful Yarns *Jazz* (wool/alpaca ④) each in #52 Ella (A) and #56 Dizzy (B)
■ 1 set (5) size 8 (5mm) double pointed needles (dpn) *or size to obtain gauge*
■ Small amounts of waste yarn

GAUGE

18 sts and 24 rows/rnds to 4"/10cm over St st using size 8 (5mm) needles.
Take time to check gauge.

CUFF PATTERN STITCH

(multiple of 4 sts)
Note Pat st is worked in rnds.
Rnd 1 *P3tog leaving sts on LH needle, yo, p same 3 sts tog again and sl from needle, k1; rep from * around.
Rnd 2 Knit.
Rnd 3 *K1, p3tog leaving sts on LH needle, yo, p same 3 sts tog again and sl from needle; rep from * around.
Rnd 4 Knit.
Rep rnds 1-4 for cuff pat st.

FIRST SOCK

CUFF

With one needle and A, cast on 48 sts. Divide sts evenly on 4 needles with 12 sts on each needle. Join, taking care not to twist sts on needles. Mark end of rnd and sl marker every rnd. Work in k2, p2 rib for 4 rnds. Then cont in cuff pat st, alternating 2 rnds A and 2 rnds B, until 24 rnds are worked in cuff pat st. Keep A & B yarns attached.
Next rnd With waste yarn, k around.
Next rnd With B, [k2, k2tog] 12 times around—9 sts rem on each of 4 needles and there are a total of 36 sts.
Work even in St st with B (k every rnd) until 5½"/14cm are worked even in St st. Change to A and k 4 rnds.

Shape toe

Next rnd *Needle 1* K1, ssk, k to end; *Needle 2* k to last 3 sts, k2tog, k1; *Needle 3* as for *Needle 1*; *Needle 4* as for *Needle 2*. Rep last rnd 4 times more—16 sts rem. Divide sts evenly onto 2 needles and weave toe sts tog using Kitchener st.

HEEL

Remove waste yarn and carefully place the 48 sts on 4 needles with 12 sts on each needle. Pm at inside corner of heel to mark beg of rnd.

Next rnd With A, *k2, k2tog; rep from * around, picking up 1 st at each inside corner of heel—38 sts.

K 1 rnd. **Next rnd Working into last st of previous rnd as first st, sl 2 sts knitwise, k1, psso, (S2KP), k to 1 st before next corner st, S2KP, k to end of rnd**.

Rep between **'s 4 times more—18 sts. Divide sts evenly onto 2 needles and weave sts tog using Kitchener st.

FINISHING

Block socks being careful not to flatten rib.

SECOND SOCK

Work as for first sock reversing colors A and B.

Girl's classic socks are topped off with a flat-knit Fair Isle cuff that folds down for added style. A length of ribbing underneath holds these socks snugly around the ankles. Designed by Debbie Bliss.

SIZES

Instructions are written for girl's size X-Small (4-5½). Changes for sizes Small (5-6½) and Medium (6-7½) are in parentheses.

KNITTED MEASUREMENTS

■ Leg width 7"/18cm
■ Foot length 4¾ (5½, 6½)"/12 (14, 16.5)cm

MATERIALS

■ 1 (1, 2) 1¾oz/50g ball (each approx 124yd/115m) of Debbie Bliss Yarns/KFI *Wool Cotton* (wool/cotton ②) in 102 beige (MC)
■ Small amounts in #606 dk red (A), #201 pale blue (B), #206 navy (C), #101 cream (D), #601 lilac (E) and #505 yellow (F)
■ One pair each sizes 2 and 3 (2.75 and 3mm) needles *or size to obtain gauge*
■ One set (4) size 3 (3mm) double pointed needles (dpn)
■ Stitch holder

GAUGE

25 sts and 34 rows/rnds to 4"/10cm over St st using larger needles.
Take time to check gauge.

Note When changing colors, twist yarn on WS to prevent holes.

CUFF

With smaller straight needles and A, cast on 49 sts. Change to MC.

Row 1 K1, *p1, k1; rep from * to end.
Row 2 P1, *k1, p1; rep from * to end.
Rep row 1 once more.
Change to larger straight needles. P 1 row.

Beg Fair Isle chart

Row 1 (RS) Work row 1 of Fair Isle chart, working 8-st rep 6 times, end with last st of chart. Cont to foll chart through row 13.
Next row (WS) With MC, purl, dec 6 sts evenly spaced across—43 sts. Change to smaller straight needles and cont with MC only. Work in k1, p1 rib for 2¼"/6cm. Change to larger needles and beg with a k row, work 4 rows in St st. Cut yarn. Change to dpn.

HEEL

Sl last 10 sts of row onto one dpn, then first 9 sts of row onto same needle—19 heel sts. Work back and forth on these heel sts only. Sl rem 24 sts to a st holder for instep. **Row 1 (RS)** With RS facing, join MC to 19 heel sts, k9, k2tog, k8, turn—18 sts. Work 9 rows in St st.

Turn heel

Next row (RS) K13, k2tog tbl, turn.
Next row Sl 1, p8, p2tog, turn.
Next row Sl 1, k8, k2tog tbl, turn.

Next row Sl 1, p8, p2tog, turn.
Rep last 2 rows until there are10 sts. Cut yarn. **Next rnd** Sl first 5 sts of needle to safety pin, pm to indicate beg of rnd, join MC and k rem 5 heel sts, then pick up and k8 sts along left side (rows) of heel, k5 instep sts (*Needle 1*—18 sts); k 14 sts of instep (*Needle 2*—14 sts); k rem 5 instep sts, pick up and k 8 sts along right side (rows) of heel k5 sts from safety pin (*Needle 3*—18 sts)—50 total sts. Join and cont in rnds as foll:

Shape instep
K 1 rnd. **Next rnd** K12, k2tog, k to last 14 sts, k2tog tbl, k12. K 1 rnd. **Next rnd** K11, k2tog, k to last 13 sts, k2tog tbl, k11. Cont to dec in this way every other rnd

having 1 less st before and after decs 3 times more—40 sts rem. Work even in St st until foot measures 3¼ (4, 5)"/8 (10, 12.5)cm from beg of heel.

Shape toe
Rnd 1 [K7, k2tog, k2, k2tog tbl, k7] twice. K 1 rnd. **Rnd 3** [K6, k2tog, k2, k2tog tbl, k6] twice. K 1 rnd. Cont to dec 4 sts every other rnd in this way (repositioning sts on needles as necessary) 3 times more—20 sts rem. Divide sts evenly onto 2 needles and weave toe sts tog using Kitchener st.

FINISHING
Block socks being careful not to flatten rib. Sew leg seams, reversing Fair Isle cuff seam for cuff turnback.

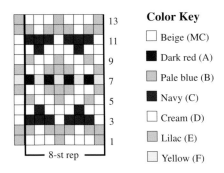

13
11
9
7
5
3
1

8-st rep

Color Key

☐ Beige (MC)

■ Dark red (A)

▨ Pale blue (B)

■ Navy (C)

☐ Cream (D)

▨ Lilac (E)

☐ Yellow (F)

MEN'S CABLE SOCKS

Socks and bonds

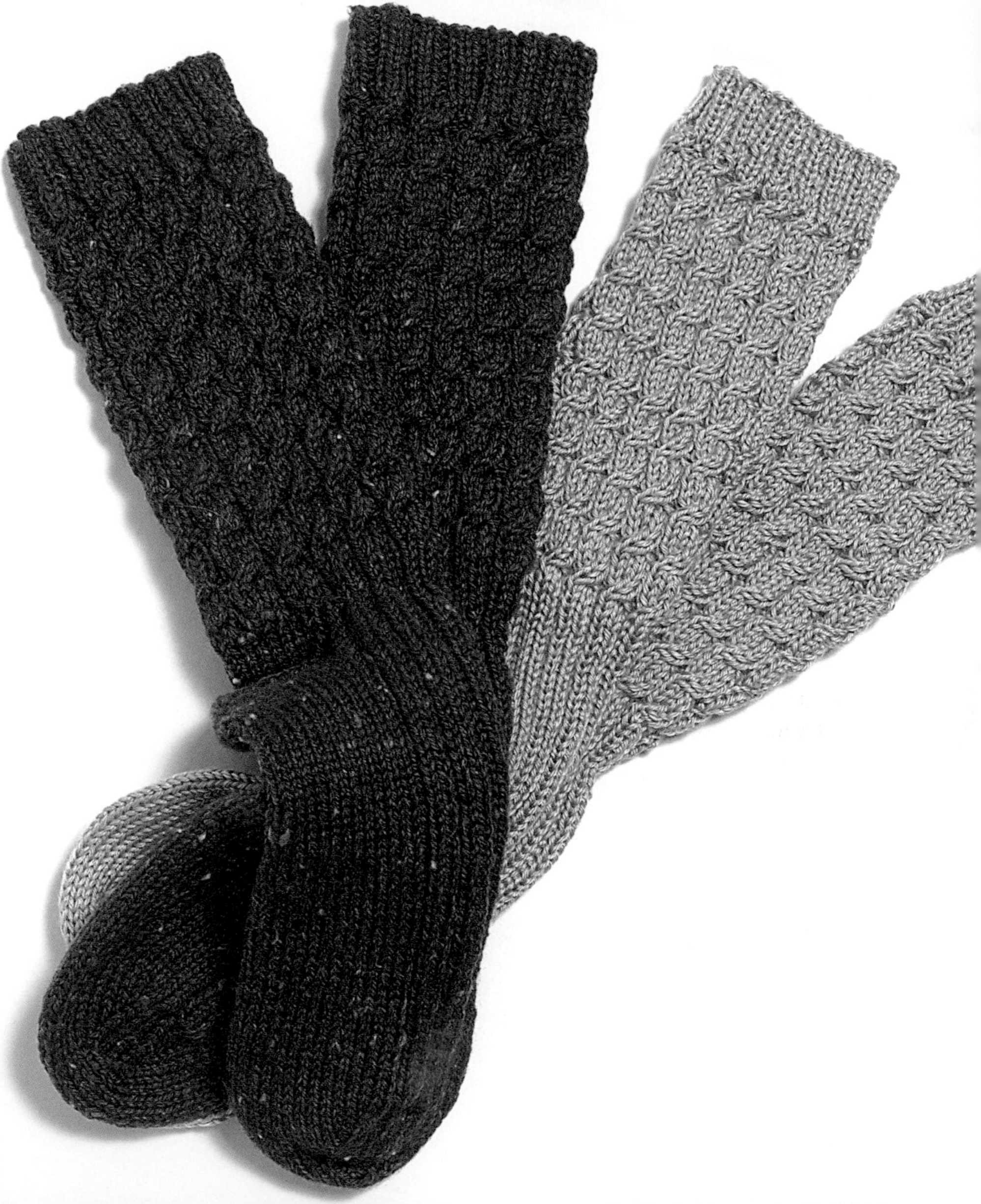

Rugged texture adds manly appeal to Jenny Bellew's easy rib-and-cable-patterned socks in lustrous or rustic wool. Knit in some elastic thread at the cuff for a snug fit.

SIZES

Instructions are written for Man's size Medium. Changes for sizes Large and X-Large are in parentheses.

KNITTED MEASUREMENTS

- Leg width 8½"/21.5cm
- Foot length 10 (11, 12)"/25.5 (28, 30.5)cm

MATERIALS

- 4 (4, 5) 1¾ oz/50g balls (each approx 108yd/100m) of Cleckheaton *Country Naturals 8-ply* by Plymouth Yarns (wool ②) in #1825 brown tweed OR
- 4 (4, 5) 1¾ oz/50g balls (each approx 99yd/92m) of Cleckheaton *Tencel Wool 8-Ply* by Plymouth Yarns (tencel/wool ②) in #2063 lt green
- One set (4) size 5 (3.75mm) double pointed needles (dpn) *or size to obtain gauge*
- Cable needle
- Elastic thread (optional)

GAUGES

- 25 sts and 31 rows/rnds to 4"/10cm over St st using size 5 (3.75mm) needles.
- 34 sts and 31 rows/rnds to 4"/10cm over cable pat using size 5 (3.75mm) needles. *Take time to check gauges.*

STITCH GLOSSARY

4-st RC Sl next 2 sts to cn and hold to *back*, k2, k2 from cn.

CUFF

Using desired yarn (plus elastic thread if desired) and one needle, cast on 64 sts. Divide sts on 3 needles having 20 sts on *Needle 1*, 20 sts on *Needle 2* and 24 sts on *Needle 3*. Join, taking care not to twist sts on needles. Mark end of rnd and sl marker every rnd.

Next rnd *K2, p2; rep from * around. Rep last rnd 9 times more, inc 8 sts evenly on last rnd—72 sts. (Cut elastic thread if necessary.) Reposition sts with 24 sts on each of 3 needles.

Beg cable pat

Rnd 1 *P2, k4; rep from * around.

Rnd 2 Rep rnd 1.

Rnd 3 *P2, 4-st RC; rep from * around.

Rnds 4-6 Rep rnd 1.

Rep rnds 1-6 for cable pat until piece measures 7½"/19cm from beg.

Next (dec) rnd *P2, k1, k2tog, k1; rep from * around—60 sts.

HEEL

Work in pat across first 15 sts, sl the last 13 sts of rnd to other end of same needle—28 heel sts. Divide the rem 32 sts onto 2 needles to be worked later for instep. **Next row** Purl, dec 6 sts evenly across—22 sts. **Next row (RS)** Sl 1 knitwise, k to end. **Next row** Sl 1 purlwise, p to end. Rep last 2 rows until there are 14 rows in heel.

Turn heel

Row 1 Sl 1, k12, k2tog, k1, turn.

Row 2 Sl 1, p5, p2tog tbl, p1, turn.

Row 3 Sl 1, k6, k2tog, k1, turn.

Row 4 Sl 1, p7, p2tog tbl, p1, turn.

Row 5 Sl 1, k8, k2tog, k1, turn.

Row 6 Sl 1, p9, p2tog tbl, p1, turn.

Row 7 Sl 1, k10, k2tog, k1, turn.

Row 8 Sl 1, p11, p2tog tbl, p1, turn—14 sts. K back across 7 sts, completing heel. Sl all instep sts onto two needles. With spare needle, k last 7 heel sts, pick up and k10 sts along side (rows) of heel (*Needle 1*), work pat in rib as established across 32 instep sts (*Needle 2*), pick up and k10 sts along other side (rows) of heel, k rem 7 heel sts (*Needle 3*)—66 total sts.

Shape instep

Rnd 1 K17 [p2, k3] 6 times, p2, k17.

Rnd 2 K14, k2tog, k1, [p2, k3] 6 times, p2, k1, SKP, k14.

Rnd 3 K16, [p2, k3] 6 times, p2, k16.

Rnd 4 K13, k2tog, k1, [p2, k3] 6 times, p2, k1, SKP, k13.

Rnd 5 K15, [p2, k3] 6 times, p2, k15.

Rnd 6 K12, k2tog, k1, [p2, k3] 6 times, p2, k1, SKP, k12. Cont to dec in this way every other rnd twice more—56 sts. Then cont to work even as established until foot measures 8½ (9½, 10½)"/21.5 (24, 26.5)cm from back of heel or 1½"/4cm less than desired length of foot.

Next rnd K12, [k2tog, k2] 8 times, k12—48 sts.

Shape toe

Rnd 1 *Needle 1* K to last 3 sts, k2tog, k1; *Needle 2* k1, SKP, k to last 3 sts, k2tog, k1; *Needle 3* k1, SKP, k to end.

Rnd 2 Knit.

Rep these 2 rnds 5 times more—24 sts rem. Divide sts evenly onto 2 needles and weave toe sts tog using Kitchener st.

FINISHING

Block socks being careful not to flatten rib.

KID'S STRIPED SOCKS

Too cool for school

Graduating, candy-colored stripes transform plain socks into a snazzy accessory. Contrasting heels and toes add decorative details to this quick-knit design by Charlotte Parry.

SIZE
Instructions are written for child's size Medium (6-7½).

KNITTED MEASUREMENTS
- Leg width 6½"/16.5cm
- Foot length 7¼"/18.5cm

MATERIALS
- 1 3½oz/100g hank (each approx 215yd/197m) of Brown Sheep Co. *Cotton Fleece* (cotton ③) each in #CW-840 green (MC-1) or #CW-210 pink (MC-2) and contrast colors in #CW-800 purple (A), #CW-340 yellow, #CW-310 orange and #CW-765 blue
- One set (4) each sizes 4 and 5 (3.5 and 3.75mm) double pointed needles (dpn) *or size to obtain gauge*

GAUGE
22 sts and 32 rows/rnds to 4"/10cm over St st using larger dpn.
Take time to check gauge.

Note Foll chart for chosen color way using lime (MC-1) or pink (MC-2) as the main color. Use the opposite MC color for the heel (see photo).

CUFF
With smaller dpn and A, loosely cast on 36 sts. Divide sts evenly on 3 needles with 12 sts on each needle. Join, taking care not to twist sts on needles. Mark end of rnd and sl marker every rnd. K 3 rnds. **Next rnd** *K2, p2; rep from * around. Cont in k2, p2 rib for 4 rnds more. Change to larger dpn. Beg with rnd 1 of stripe chart, work in St st and stripe pat using chosen colors, through rnd 40. Leg measures approx 6"/15cm from beg. Cut yarn.

HEEL
Sl first 9 sts of *Needle 1* onto spare needle, then sl last 9 sts of *Needle 2* onto other end of same needle—18 heel sts. Divide rem 18 sts onto 2 needles for instep to be worked later. Work back and forth in rows on the 18 heel sts only. **Row 1 (RS)** Join MC-1 (or MC-2), k18 heel sts. Cont in St st for a total of 1"/2.5cm, end with a RS row.

Turn heel
Row 1 (WS) Sl 1, p9, p2tog, p1, turn. **Row 2** Sl 1, k3, k2tog, k1, turn. **Row 3** Sl 1, p4, p2tog, p1, turn. **Row 4** Sl 1, k5, k2tog, k1, turn. **Row 5** Sl 1, p6, p2tog, p1, turn. **Row 6** Sl 1, k7, k2tog, k1—10 sts. **Row 7** Sl 1, p8, p2tog, turn. **Row 8** Sl 1, k8, k2tog, turn. Cut yarn. **Next rnd** Sl last 5 sts of heel to *Needle 1* and with MC-1 or MC-2, k5, then cont with MC, pick up and k11 sts along left side (rows) of heel (16 sts—*Needle 1*); k next 18 sts for instep (*Needle 2*); pick up and k11 sts along right

side of heel, k5 from rem heel sts (16 *Needle 3*) and a total of 50 sts. Beg with row 42, cont in stripe pat and work as foll:

Shape instep

Rnd 1 Knit. **Rnd 2** *Needle 1* K to last 3 sts, k2tog, k1; *Needle 2* knit; *Needle 3* k1, SKP, k to end. Rep last 2 rnds 6 times more—36 sts. Cont in stripe pat through rnd 79 or until foot measures 6¼"/16cm from beg of heel. Change to A.

Shape toe

Rnd 1 *Needle 1* K to last 3 sts, k2tog, k1; *Needle 2* k1, SKP, k to last 3 sts, k2tog, k1; *Needle 3* k1, SKP, k to end. **Rnd 2** Knit. Rep last 2 rnds 3 times more—20 sts. Divide sts evenly onto 2 needles and weave toe sts tog using Kitchener st.

FINISHING

Block socks being careful not to flatten rib.

GREEN SOCK   **PINK SOCK**

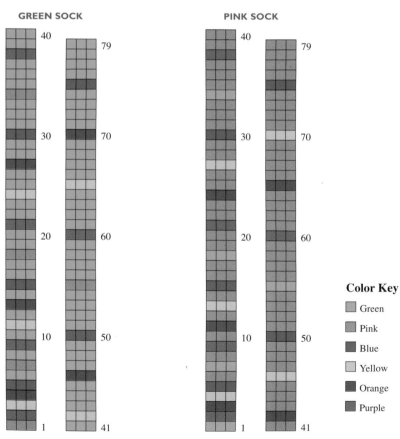

Color Key

- Green
- Pink
- Blue
- Yellow
- Orange
- Purple

MEDIEVAL KNEE SOCKS

Italian artisan

Inspired by a pair of red silk stockings found in the tomb of Eleanora de Toledo on display in the Palazzo Pitti Museum in Florence, these socks represent one of the earliest documented examples of lace in knitting. Designed and interpreted by Margaret Stove.

SIZE

Instructions are written for Woman's size Medium/Large.

KNITTED MEASUREMENTS

- Leg width 10½"/26.5cm
- Foot length 8½"/21.5cm

MATERIALS

- 5 1¾oz/50g balls (each approx 112yd/ 104m) of Naturally/S.R. Kertzer *Luxury DK* (wool/mohair ④) in #933 cranberry
- 1 set (5) size 5 (3.75mm) double pointed needles (dpn) *or size to obtain gauge*

GAUGE

23 sts and 28 rows/rnds to 4"/10cm over St st using size 5 (3.75mm) dpn.
Take time to check gauge.

CUFF

Using one needle, cast on 60 sts. Divide sts on 3 needles with 20 sts on each needle. Join, taking care not to twist sts on needles. Mark end of rnd and sl marker every rnd.

Beg chart 1

Rnd 1 Purl. Cont to foll chart in this way through rnd 68. Then rep rnds 69-72 a total of 6 times. Then work rnds 93 and 94 foll chart—there are 54 sts.

Eyelet rnd—Rnd 95 Foll rnd 95 of chart. Then work rnds 96-100 foll chart.

Shape heel seams

Note Foll chart or work as foll:

Rnd 101 M1, ssk, work pat to last 3 sts, k2tog, M1, p1.

Rnd 102 K2, pat to last 3 sts, k3.

Rnd 103 M1, p1, ssk, work pat to last 4 sts, k2tog, p1, M1, k1.

Rnd 104 K3, pat to last 4 sts, k4.

Rnd 105 M1, k1, p1, ssk, work pat to last 5 sts, k2tog, p1, k1, M1, k1.

Rnd 106 P1, k3, work pat to last 5 sts, k3, p1, k1.

Rnd 107 M1, p1, k1, p1, ssk, work pat to last 6 sts, k2tog, p1, k1, p1, M1, k1.

Rnd 108 K1, p1, k3, work pat to last 6 sts, k3, p1, k2.

Rnd 109 K1, M1, p1, k1, p1, ssk, work pat to last 7 sts, k2tog, p1, k1, p1, M1, k2.

Rnd 110 K2, p1, k3, work pat to last 7 sts, k3, p1, k3.

Rnd 111 K2, M1, p1, k1, p1, ssk, work pat to last 8 sts, k2tog, p1, k1, p1, M1, k3.

Rnd 112 K3, p1, k3, work pat to last 8 sts, k3, p1, k4.

Rnd 113 K3, M1, p1, k1, p1, ssk, work pat to last 9 sts, k2tog, p1, k1, p1, M1, k4.

Rnd 114 K4, p1, k3, work pat to last 9 sts, k3, p1, k5.

Rnd 115 K3, M1, [k1, p1] twice, ssk, work pat to last 10 sts, k2tog, [p1, k1] twice, M1, k4.

Rnd 116 K5, p1, k3, work pat to last 10 sts, k3, p1, k6.

Rnd 117 K3, M1, k2, p1, k1, p1, ssk, work pat to last 11 sts, k2tog, p1, k1, p1, k2, M1, k4.

Rnd 118 K6, p1, k3, work pat to last 11 sts, k3, p1, k7.

Rnd 119 K3, M1, k3, p1, k1, p1, ssk, work pat to last 12 sts, k2tog, p1, k1, p1, k3, M1, k4.

Rnd 120 K7, p1, k3, work pat to last 12 sts, k3, p1, k8.

Rnd 121 K3, M1, k4, p1, k1, p1, ssk, work pat to last 13 sts, k2tog, p1, k1, p1, k4, M1, k4.

Rnd 122 K8, p1, k3, work pat to last 13 sts, k3, p1, k9.

Rnd 123 K3, M1, k5, p1, k1, p1, ssk, work pat to last 14 sts, k2tog, p1, k1, p1, k5, M1, k4.

Rnd 124 K9, p1, k3, work pat to last 14 sts, k3, p1, k10.

Rnd 125 K3, M1, k6, p1, k1, p1, ssk, work pat to last 15 sts, k2tog, p1, k1, p1, k6, M1, k4.

Rnd 126 K10, p1, k3, work pat to last 15 sts, k3, p1, k11.

Turn heel

Sl first 13 sts of *Needle 1* to spare needle, sl next 27 sts onto 2 needles for instep to be worked later, then leave the 14 sts from *Needle 3* on a separate needle for heel—27 heel sts.

Row 1 Beg with the last 13 sts of heel, k3, turn. **Row 2** P7, turn. **Row 3** K7, then k next st tog with left side "turning" st of previous row to prevent hole, turn. **Row 4** P8, then p next st tog with the left side turning st of previous row, turn. (Cont in this way through the short rows to turn heel). **Row 5** K10, turn. **Row 6** P11, turn. **Row 7** K12, turn. Cont to work short rows in this way adding 1 st each row 8 times more. **Row 16** P21, turn. **Row 17** K21, p1, turn. **Row 18** K1, p21, k1, turn. **Row 19** P1, k21, p1, k1, p1, turn. **Row 20** P2, k1, p21, purl picked-up lp then place on LH needle, pass next unworked st over this st and sl back to RH needle, k1, turn. **Row 21** K2, p1, k11. End of heel shaping. Cont to foll chart 2, work rnds 1 and 2. Then rep rnds 3-6 a total of 8 times.

Shape toe

Rnd 35 Beg at center of sole, k8, ssk, p1, work 7 sts in pat, ssk, work 13 sts in pat, k2tog, work 7 sts in pat, p1, k2tog, k9.

Next and all even rnds Work even in pat.

Rnd 37 K7, ssk, p1, work 7 sts in pat, ssk, work 11 sts in pat, k2tog, work 7 sts in pat, p1, k2tog, k8.

Rnd 39 K6, ssk, p1, work 7 sts in pat, ssk, work 9 sts in pat, k2tog, work 7 sts in pat, p1, k2tog, k3.

Cont to work in this way through rnd 46.

Rnd 47 K2, ssk, p1, work 7 sts in pat, ssk, p1, k2tog, work 7 sts in pat, p1, k2tog, k3—26 sts.

Next rnd K3, [k2tog] twice, p2tog, [ssk] twice, k1, k2tog, p2tog, [ssk] twice, k2, k2tog—16 sts. Divide sts evenly on 2 needles and weave toe sts tog using Kitchener st.

FINISHING

Block socks being careful not to flatten. Make two 30"/75cm twisted cords and draw through eyelet rnds on socks.

Twisted cord

1 If you have someone to help you, insert a pencil or knitting needle through each end of the strands. If not, place one end over a doorknob and put a pencil through the other end. Turn the strands clockwise until they are tightly twisted.

2 Keeping the strands taut, fold the piece in half. Remove the pencils and allow the cords to twist onto themselves.

Stitch Key

☐ K on RS, p on WS

— P on RS, k on WS

◩ K2tog

◪ P2tog

O Yo

◪ Ssk

◻ M 1

◪ SK2P

▨ No stitches or stitches left unworked

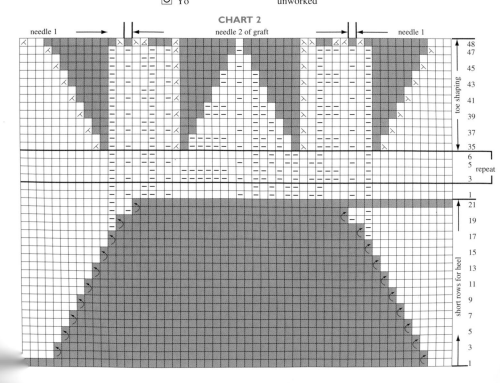

CHART 2

CHART 1

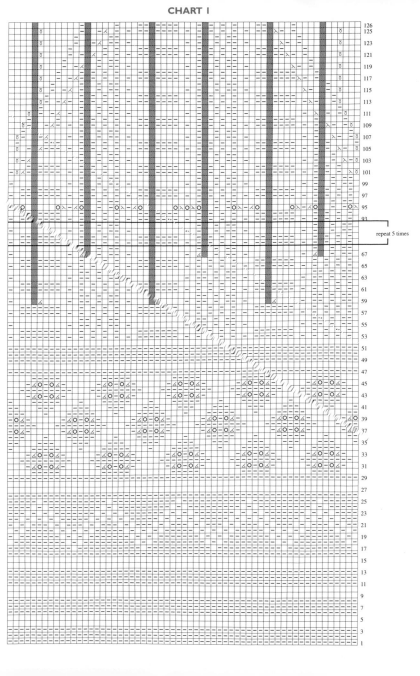

repeat 5 times

RESOURCES

US RESOURCES

Write to the yarn companies listed below for purchasing and mail-order information.

ARTFUL YARNS
distributed by
JCA

BERROCO, INC.
PO Box 367
Uxbridge, MA 01569

BROWN SPEEP CO.
100662 County Road 16
Mitchell, NE 69357

CLASSIC ELITE YARNS
300A Jackson Street
Lowell, MA 01852

CLECKHEATON
distributed by
Plymouth Yarn

DEBBIE BLISS YARN
distributed by
Knitting Fever, Inc.

FILATURA DI CROSA
distributed by
Tahki•Stacy Charles, Inc.

GGH
distributed by
Muench Yarns

JCA
35 Scales Lane
Townsend, MA 01469

KI C2, LLC
2220 Eastman Avenue #105
Ventura, CA 93003

KNITTING FEVER, INC.
P. O. Box 502
Roosevelt, NY 11575

KOIGU WOOL DESIGNS
R R #1
Williamsford, ON N0H 2V0
Canada

LANE BORGOSESIA
PO Box 217
Colorado Springs, CO 80903

LANG
distributed by
Berroco, Inc.

LION BRAND YARN CO.
34 West 15 St.
New York, NY 10011

LORNA'S LACES YARNS
P. O. Box 795
Somerset, CA 95684

MUENCH YARNS
285 Bel Marin Keys Blvd.
Unit J
Novato, CA 94949-5724

NATURALLY
distributed by
S. R. Kertzer, Ltd.

PATONS®
PO Box 40
Listowel, ON
N4W 3H3
Canada

PLYMOUTH YARN
PO Box 28
Bristol, PA 19007

ROWAN YARNS
5 Northern Blvd.
Amherst, NH 03031

S. R. KERTZER, LTD.
105A Winges Road
Woodbridge, ON L4L 6C2
Canada

STAHL WOLLE
distirbuted by
Tahki • Stacy Charles, Inc.

TAHKI•STACY CHARLES, INC.
8000 Cooper Ave.
Glendale, NY 11385

VOGUE KNITTING SOCKS TWO

Editor-in-Chief
TRISHA MALCOLM

Art Director
CHI LING MOY

Executive Editor
CARLA S. SCOTT

Instructions Editor
MARI LYNN PATRICK

Knitting Editor
JEAN GUIRGUIS

Yarn Editor
VERONICA MANNO

Editorial Coordinator
MICHELLE LO

Photography
**EYE[4]MEDIA
BOBB CONNORS**

Book Manager
THERESA MCKEON

Production Manager
DAVID JOINNIDES

■

President, Sixth&Spring Books
ART JOINNIDES

LOOK FOR THESE OTHER TITLES IN
THE VOGUE ON THE GO SERIES...

■

CANADIAN RESOURCES

Write to US resources for mail-order availability of yarns not listed.

BERROCO, INC.
distributed by
S. R. Kertzer, Ltd.

CLASSIC ELITE YARNS
distributed by
S. R. Kertzer, Ltd.

DIAMOND YARN
9697 St. Laurent
Montreal, PQ H3L 2N1
and

155 Martin Ross, Unit #3
Toronto, ON M3J 2L9

ESTELLE DESIGNS & SALES, LTD.
Units 65/67
2220 Midland Ave.
Scarborough, ON M1P 3E6

KOIGU WOOL DESIGNS
R R #1
Williamsford, ON N0H 2V0

LANG
distributed by
Estelle Designs & Sales, Ltd.

NATURALLY
distributed by
S. R. Kertzer, Ltd.

PATONS ®
PO Box 40
Listowel, ON N4W 3H3

ROWAN
distributed by
Diamond Yarn

S. R. KERTZER, LTD.
105A Winges Rd.
Woodbridge, ON L4L 6C2

UK RESOURCES

Not all yarns used in this book are available in the UK. For yarns not available, make a comparable substitute or contact the US manufacturer for purchasing and mail-order information.

ROWAN YARNS
Green Lane Mill
Holmfirth
West Yorks HD7 1RW
Tel: 01484-681881

SILKSTONE
12 Market Place
Cockermouth
Cumbria, CA13 9NQ
Tel: 01900-821052

THOMAS RAMSDEN GROUP
Netherfield Road
Guiseley
West Yorks LS20 9PD
Tel: 01943-872264